CHOOSE YOUR BEST LIFE

How to Use Your Personality Type to Conquer Self-Doubt in Times of Change, Transition, and Important Life Decisions

GARY WILLIAMS

Copyright © 2019 by Gary Williams

All rights reserved. No part of this publication may be reproduced, distributed, or transmitted in any form or by any means, including photocopying, recording, or other electronic or mechanical methods, without the prior written permission of the publisher, except in the case of brief quotations embodied in critical reviews and certain other uses permitted by copyright law.

Although the author has made every effort to ensure that the information in this book was correct at press time, the author and publisher do not assume and hereby disclaim any liability to any party for any loss, damage, or disruption caused by errors or omissions, whether such errors or omissions result from negligence, accident, or any other cause.

The resources in this book are provided for informational purposes only and should not be used to replace the specialized training and professional judgment of a health care or mental health care professional. Neither the author nor the publisher can be held responsible for the use of the information provided within this book. Please always consult a trained professional before making any decision regarding treatment of yourself or others.

Choose Your Best Life: How to Use Your Personality Type to Conquer Self-Doubt in Times of Change, Transition, and Important Life Decisions —1st ed.

ISBN 978-1-7340160-0-0

Published by Better Future Publishing

Table of Contents

Download Your Free Workbook	4
Mediocrity or Your Best Life	7
Setting the Stage	17
Doubt	35
Stress	53
Your Individual Uniqueness	65
Your Energy	77
Understanding	89
Choice	101
Structure	115
Synergy	125
What's Next?	139

Download Your Free Workbook Now!

As a gift to my readers to help you get the most of this book, I encourage you to download a FREE workbook to use alongside this book.

I believe that being actively engaged in any journey is critical to get the most out of the experience. This workbook will give you space to stop and think about critical points you'll discover throughout this book.

Go to
www.betterfuturecoaching.com/CYBLworkbook
to download your FREE workbook today!

This book is dedicated to the people in my life that are consistently challenging me to see my individual uniqueness and live out of that space on a daily basis.

CHAPTER 1

Mediocrity or Your Best Life– Which Will You Choose?

In our socially connected online world, seeing the life highlight reel of others often causes self-doubt. When was the last time you saw pictures of someone you know on social media and instantly started comparing yourself to the life they seem to be living? This comparison can often leave you spiraling out internally, experiencing self-doubt, and feeling stuck and overwhelmed.

In this period of your life, you are often faced with critical life decisions that can impact the trajectory of your life. Which job will you take? Where will you live? Who should you marry? These transitions and important life decisions can often result in you feeling overwhelmed—not knowing how to take action because you don't know what to do. This overwhelm is causing you to doubt yourself, which is ultimately limiting you from living your best life.

> *They [millennials] think that they're supposed to come out of college and have their brand ... how I got to be a brand was not trying to be a brand! How I got to be a brand was: every day, making choices that felt like 'this is the right move' and 'now that's the next right move.'*
>
> —Oprah Winfrey

In this book, I will show you how to overcome self-doubt through discovering what makes your mind unique. By understanding your uniqueness, you'll then be able to make choices that allow you to operate out of your natural and authentic self. A series of choices resulting in one "right move" at a time will begin to shape the life that you were meant to live. The measuring stick of your best life must come from you internally, not the outside expectations of the world. This self-discovery will allow you to make the choice to live your best life out of your own potential, instead of a life of mediocrity based on the expectations of others.

Perhaps, there have been too many times when seeing the success of others causes you to compare your life to theirs, sparking self-doubt within you. In this book, you will discover what makes you unique so that you can begin to craft your own unique life through choosing one "right move" at a time. This will allow you to take action from a place of inner confidence by embracing the unique way you think, feel, and act, instead of feeling frozen by the overwhelm of self-doubt.

A World of Standardization

We are living in a world that values standardization over the unique and beautiful individuality within each of us. This is one of my greatest frustrations with our education system. Educational curriculum and student learning are based on one commonality: the student's year of birth. Students advance from one grade to the next as a cohort based off of their age, and are all compared against one another based off of their academic performance (grades) and standardized tests. This is evidence that our education system has a focus on standardizing the experience for all students, instead of embracing the uniqueness each student brings to the table.

When is it that we explicitly teach students to learn about themselves, about how they think and feel, or about the way that their particular mind influences their behavior? From my experience, we don't. You may learn some of this as an outcome of extracurricular activities or transformational teachers that go above and beyond, but it is not part of the explicit educational curriculum. As a result of the era of standardized tests, students are measured via comparison to their peers, instead of identifying and promoting each's individual strengths, interests, and potential.

My professional journey began in the world of public education as a middle school teacher, later serving as an instructional coach for teachers. I have facilitated leadership development conferences, workshops, and trainings, domestically and internationally, as a result of my fascination with human behavior and the individual uniqueness of others. I have personally sparked conversations with thousands of people that have allowed them to discover how their uniqueness can liberate them to live a more meaningful life. Although I've had the privilege to influence many people over the years, it's simply not enough. This is my inspiration for this book. It's time for you to conquer self-doubt through discovering your individual uniqueness. This self-discovery will instill you with the confidence and the tools to choose your best life.

Discovering Your Uniqueness

In this book, I will apply the work of Carl Jung that was later developed into the Myers-Briggs Type Indicator® with a lens that is easy to understand and will increase your self-awareness. As a Certified Practitioner of the Myers-Briggs Type Indicator (MBTI® instrument), I have personally supported thousands of high school and college students, teachers, business people, and other young professionals in deepening their understanding of their own individual uniqueness.

Please note, if you already have a thorough understanding of the Myers-Briggs Type Indicator and you're looking for a personal development book that goes deep into each of the sixteen types, this book may not be for you. This book has been crafted to look at the tool as a lens to overcome self-doubt, but this book will not go into descriptions of each of the sixteen personality types. If you're not familiar with the tool, or would like to explore how to apply the framework to overcome self-doubt and choose your best life, then this book is certainly for you.

> *Your vision will become clear only when you can look into your own heart. Who looks outside, dreams; who looks inside, awakes.*
>
> *—Carl Jung*

With this book I invite you to embark on this journey of discovering yourself to a greater depth. This self-discovery will move you from a place of being stuck in self-doubt to, instead, seeing that you have a choice to live the best version of your life. Many people in their twenties and thirties have been able to overcome a sense of self-doubt by working with me to help them discover with greater clarity their individual uniqueness, their individual preferences, and their personality type—you can become one of those people as well.

Trisha, a young professional who has pushed through doubt by discovering her uniqueness says, *"Gary has constantly been someone who has encouraged me to stop and think. Gary pushes me to stay true to who I am, which includes using my strengths and personality traits that help make the world a better place. Gary's ability to work with me in times of uncertainty has allowed me to feel confident in tough decisions. I am so thankful for his guidance and never-ending compassion when facing tough decisions. He is truly someone who wants me to be the best I can be and will help me in whatever way he can."*

In this book, you will gain a deeper understanding of what makes you unique. This self-discovery will allow you to see ways to create a better sense of balance in your life by living authentically. Ultimately, this will help you move from self-doubt to making a series of choices in your life that will liberate you to live the best version of your life.

If you're content with experiencing self-doubt and living a life of status quo, this book is definitely not for you. Don't be the person that loses out on a lifetime full of adventure, just because you're letting self-doubt stop you from taking action. This book will give you a framework to discover your uniqueness in a way that can help you maneuver change, transition, and important life decisions by perceiving them with a positive outlook, rather than being frozen in fear.

Every human being has a unique wiring of their mind that influences the way they think, act, and behave. We rarely take time to think about our own individual uniqueness because it is second nature to us. Our own minds are all we've ever known and experienced, so it can sometimes be hard to identify and then capitalize on the things that make us unique.

The number one goal of this book is to help you overcome self-doubt and help you through important life decisions by first understanding what makes you unique. In this book, we will first explore how changes and transitions in your life often spark self-doubt. Then, we will explore the importance of understanding who you are as an individual and what makes you unique. Finally, we will begin to see how to create a greater sense of balance in your life, moving from a place of self-doubt to viewing the world around you—including the changes, transitions, important life decisions, and challenges you face—as a series of choices that can result in you living the best version of your life.

Tools to Choose Your Best Life

Throughout this book there several recurring tools that you will encounter that are designed to support you in the journey of applying the concepts in an engaging and meaningful way.

1. **Doubt in the Wild:** In order to reach the conclusions I've made about self-doubt, I conducted a survey that was inclusive of fifty respondents between the ages of 20 and 47. "Doubt in the Wild" offers quotes from the stories shared by the survey respondents. Their prompt was to explain a

specific moment they experienced doubt in their twenties or thirties.

2. **Stop & Think:** These are reflection questions to support you in the process of self-discovery at the end of each chapter. These questions are designed to help you engage in the given material in a meaningful way.

3. **Free Digital Workbook Download:** At the beginning of this book, I invited you to download a *free digital workbook* to help you stay actively engaged with the content. As a teacher, I refused to let my students be passive participants in the classroom. It is important to make a conscious effort to think and apply what you're learning in a book of this nature. I invite you to download the free workbook to write out answers to questions posed throughout this book in order to get the most out of this experience.

4. **A Story of Choice:** Between each chapter in this book, you will find a section titled "A Story of Choice" designed to give you an in-depth reflection from one of the respondents of the survey mentioned above. Each story will include a direct response of when that individual experienced doubt in their twenties or thirties, a description of when they're at their best, and a brief commentary from me.

Each of these components are strategically designed to help bring the concepts described in this book to life. It's my goal to include these tools to help you on the journey of moving from doubt to discovery, so that you can ultimately live your best life.

If you'd like to live a life of status quo, stop reading now. Really, I'm not offended ... This book isn't for everyone.

If you'd rather go down the path of discovering your individual uniqueness with greater clarity, then let's embark on this journey together by making the choice to continue together now.

Stop & Think

1. When do you notice that you compare yourself to others the most?

2. What's an important life decision you've recently made? When did you notice yourself feeling overwhelmed or doubting the decision?

3. You've been given a choice of either living a life of status quo or living your best life . . . which will you choose?

A Story of Choice

Enjoy the following thoughts from Katie R. (age 23), sharing when she experiences doubt and when she's at her best.

Doubt in the Wild

I know I'm experiencing self-doubt right now, while I'm in graduate school. It's like a roller coaster of "I love this and I'm doing the right thing" to "No, actually, I don't know why I'm even here." You could say I had a similar experience in my undergraduate studies, but it was definitely easier to get out of the feeling of self-doubt because I could just try out a new major . . . or five. But in graduate school, I think the feeling of being stuck to this one area of study can bring on some self-doubt.

Discover You at Your Best

I am at my best when I am able to utilize my strengths to create some form of positive change. For example, in my undergraduate studies I participated and led multiple alternative breaks—a weeklong trip for college students to engage in serving others. Going on a service trip with 11 other college students may not be everyone's cup of tea, but it was my absolute favorite time of the school year. To spend my time understanding an issue in this world, to travel to a new place, and to utilize my strengths to help people, animals, or the environment brings me so much joy. These alternative breaks also helped me question our world and think about where I could see myself fitting in it. Being a part of something greater than myself helps me feel significant.

Reflections from Gary

In these thoughts from Katie, we are able to see how a common important life decision impacted her internally. Choosing a college major or entering into a graduate program can be an amazing opportunity to choose your best life, but it can also cause self-doubt if you're not entirely sure what path you want to take. This is an experience shared by so many college students as they begin thinking about their place in the world. At her best, we see Katie's love for exploring new places, serving others, and understanding problems in our world. Katie mentioned that when she had the opportunity to utilize her strengths, she was able to feel like she was at her best. In this book, I would also challenge *you* to consider what your unique strengths are. Knowing your strengths, a key part of what makes you unique, can allow you to experience the same sense of joy described by Katie. Let's continue on to learn more about what makes you unique.

CHAPTER 2

Setting the Stage

Preparing for the Future of Change

Hundreds of years ago, many aspects of life were harder for our ancestors, but arguably much less complicated. Today, our lives are busy, full of hustle and bustle, and filled with so much change. These changes and transitions can be incredibly powerful, simply because they allow us to stretch, grow, and develop. However, today's fast-paced lifestyle can leave many feeling overwhelmed with self-doubt.

In your twenties and thirties, you are surrounded by more changes and transitions than any other time period of your life. Those changes and transitions impact every facet of your life. Think about it, when graduating from high school, you are forced to make a choice. What is it that you will do next in your one and only life?

After graduating from high school, many people decide to pursue some form of higher education, continuing to gain the skills needed for future jobs. This might be in the form of technical training, an associate's degree, or a bachelor's degree. Even with furthering your education, it can be challenging to feel confident with your future job, as experts from the Institute for the Future estimated in 2017 that 85% of the jobs that today's students will be doing in 2030 don't yet exist.

Even if you make the choice to continue your education, it can still be incredibly challenging to determine what it is that you actually want to do with your life. I have seen firsthand many new college students struggle to determine their college major or clearly articulate their future goals.

Doubt in the Wild
I feel like I am constantly in doubt. Especially in college, I always wondered if what I was doing was the path that was best for me. Now that I am in a specific career, I wonder about my future in this career, when to start a family, etc.
—Sam N. (age 25)

Transitioning in the Workplace

Some people make the choice to enter straight into the workforce, finding a job that interests them or one that will simply pay the bills. Sometimes at this stage in life, survival is more important than anything else.

Feeling the need to survive financially may have stemmed from our life experiences. Collectively, we experienced the pain of the

2008 economic crisis, often referred to as the worst economic crash since the Great Depression of 1929. This crisis is certainly enough to create uncertainty when selecting jobs and making major financial decisions.

Regardless of what path you end up picking, you will eventually have to pick jobs that you want to apply for. Again, this can be an incredibly challenging decision for so many people. Finding jobs that are interesting to you, that will pay enough to survive, and that you're actually qualified for can be incredibly challenging when you're first entering the workforce.

Even after landing that first job, so many people face additional work-related transitions in the early stages of their careers. It is likely that you will switch jobs within the first few years. According to the US Bureau of Labor Statistics, most Americans born in the early 1980s, on average, held 7.8 different jobs between the ages of eighteen to thirty years old. Again, the reason people change jobs so early in their careers often varies from person to person. However, it is likely that when you are looking for a new job, it could be to make more money, because of disagreements with your supervisors or coworkers, to move up in your career, or simply because you don't like your job.

How are you ever supposed to feel confident as a young professional knowing that you will likely pursue many different jobs?

You might be tempted to not only find a new job, but to enter into an entirely different career path. After a short while in your first job, you might realize that it just wasn't what you were hoping for. This can often be enough for a person to reconsider the decisions they have made thus far in their life and hop over to a job that's completely different.

How can you ever be sure that you're in the "right" job?

> **Doubt in the Wild**
> *I experienced doubt when changing careers. I wasn't feeling confident in my abilities and if they would be fully understood by my new team. Not receiving recognition from my colleagues, superiors, or friends causes me to compile doubts.*
> *—Dillon B. (age 27)*

Relationships

Another huge aspect of life for people in their twenties and thirties is a focus on relationships. Many relationships will shift in priority throughout this period of life, either as a result of external changes in your life or as a result of a shift in internal values.

We, as human beings, are tribal creatures. We are meant to live in community with others. Relationships are part of who we are as a species. Although relationships are essential, it's likely that in this period of our lives, our relationships are changing and can spark self-doubt.

Friendships

It is not uncommon for people to have a shift in relationships when they graduate from high school simply because there are a lot of changes that occur at this point in life. For many people, they are moving out of their family's home in order to go to school.

Even if you aren't moving away, it is likely some of your friends or people you know are moving away in this period. These changes can cause a shift in who it is that you're choosing to surround yourself with.

If you head off to college, it is not uncommon to try and quickly find new friends if you have moved away to someplace new. By nature, we are social beings. We are hardwired as human beings to live in community. Moving away from who you have known your entire life will quickly influence you to try and find new social connections in your new environment.

Even if you make the choice to stay where you've always grown up, it is not uncommon to have changes in friend groups simply because you're growing older or people are moving away. These changes can influence us to seek out new social circles or add people into our existing social circles.

Our friends can be a fundamental part of how we see ourselves. Jim Rohn is often credited with saying, "You're the average of the five people you spend the most time with." If your friendships are constantly changing, the way you see yourself is likely going to change too. Sometimes this causes us to question who we are hanging out with. Other times this can cause us to question our own identity.

Whether your friendships are changing or remaining relatively stable, it is likely social media is impacting the way you see yourself and others. While scrolling through my Facebook and Instagram accounts (when I really should have been writing this book), I observed posts from friends doing mission work in Thailand and Ghana, a celebratory post of a friend receiving her PhD, a couple that I went to high school with celebrating their first home, and a friend who will now be making a six-figure salary due to his new promotion.

Maybe it's just me, but when I see posts like these on social media, I find thoughts flying through my mind a mile a minute: "That looks more exciting than what I'm doing. Wow, they seem like they're making a difference. I wish I could find a way to make that much money . . ." I find myself comparing my life to the highlight reels of my friends. I find myself questioning the decisions I've made that have led me to this very point in time. I find doubt creeping into my mind, and this causes me stress and anxiousness.

Family

It is common for these life changes and transitions to influence the way we view and interact with our families. It is not uncommon for people to become closer to their immediate family in their twenties and thirties as a result of moving out of the same house.

In this context, it is common for some people to find that moving away from their family allows them to value what is truly great about their family. When living together for such a long time period, it is easy to get overly critical of day-to-day annoyances, and many people find that moving away is a healthy change.

In contrast, it is also common for some people to grow farther apart from their families. When you get the opportunity to move away from your family, it is quite possible that you simply do not get to see them as much as you are used to. This can sometimes cause a strain in familial relationships.

Finally, moving away from family can sometimes have a detrimental impact on us personally, and many people face some degree of "homesickness." The change of moving away from home can cause you to miss the day-to-day norms that you are used to. The change in physical location can often cause you to miss the way things used to be, and that's totally normal.

Family often creates a sense of security through the foundation that has been present in our lives. Whether you had an amazing experience growing up with your family, or the furthest thing from it, you've likely been able to rely on your family or those closest to you in some hard times in your life.

I personally have been reliant on my parents for health insurance, which is something so important to me. At the age of five, I was diagnosed with type 1 diabetes. I quite frankly have an expensive cost of living as a result of this diagnosis. Luckily, I was able to maintain health insurance through my parents until the age of 26, but transitioning through this has been a challenge. My dependency on insurance through my parents has now made me appreciate them so much more. However, the reality of this transition causes so much uncertainty for me. Finding my own health insurance has proven to be incredibly expensive, and the coverage isn't as thorough as what I'm used to. My family provided an amazing foundation for me growing up, but the uncertainty for my own health coverage has left me feeling uneasy.

I imagine you've been dependent on your family or those closest to you for something major in your life as well. As you grow older, I wouldn't be surprised if you've shared that experience that I described for myself—something you've depended on for years is suddenly becoming harder to navigate or the same level of support just isn't present. Perhaps you can relate to that uneasy feeling as a result of uncertainty when something you've depended on, such as your family or health insurance, begins to change.

Romantic Relationships

Many people in their twenties and thirties begin to prioritize romantic relationships. The prioritization of romantic relationships is often primarily driven either internally or externally.

For some people, they really value having a companion or significant other. This internal value system is a motivating factor to initiate a relationship with others. For other people, they feel external pressures to begin developing a relationship with someone that could be their life partner.

The way that we initiate relationships today is certainly different than previous generations. Technology has changed the way that people seek and develop romantic relationships. In the era of "swiping right" to find your match on dozens of dating applications, you would think that finding a romantic relationship would be easier than ever! Unfortunately, this isn't always the case.

According to American psychologist Barry Schwartz in his book *The Paradox of Choice*, "Having too many choices produces psychological distress, especially when combined with regret, concern about status, adaptation, social comparison, and perhaps most important, the desire to have the best of everything—to maximize."

In the context of romantic relationships, the increase in options of possible partners can actually decrease satisfaction, cause negative perceptions of the decision, and cause unpleasant emotions.

In addition to an increase in the number of options, I've heard multiple stories of people "swiping right" and going out on a first date with someone they really thought would be the one they'd ultimately marry. The same individuals later report being ghosted after the first date.

The feeling of rejection can be incredibly detrimental to how we see ourselves. I've had numerous conversations with others who end up believing that they are not worthy of love or that they'll never find a partner to eventually marry. This sense of rejection can make us experience self-doubt in a way that can even be detrimental to future relationships.

Another frequent narrative I hear, especially amongst many women, is the need to find a partner, get married, and have kids before their biological clock expires. This is a conversation I frequently hear as single women begin to approach their thirties and beyond. This pressure that women experience is something I will never fully understand as a man, but I have personally witnessed many women in my life burst out into tears as a result of the emotional pain caused by this reality. This pain can cause women in particular to doubt themselves, which really begins to influence the way they see themselves.

Parenting

It's not uncommon for many people in their twenties and thirties to prioritize starting a family. The reality is, becoming a parent is a huge life change. It impacts every area of your life, and it can feel like a lot of pressure to raise another human in our world.

Not only can the pressure of wanting to raise a family be an extreme source of doubt, but so can becoming a first-time parent. When talking with several friends who have recently become parents, I often hear about the overwhelming love they have for their newborn child. I also often hear negative self-talk about their ability to raise a child.

> **Doubt in the Wild**
> *Motherhood. Every day is a new doubt. Am I doing it "right"? Will he grow up to be a respectful man? Will he ever sleep through the night? Am I setting him up for failure? Will he meet all of his milestones? Am I cut out for this?! The list goes on and on . . .*
>
> *—Erica V. (age 25)*

Self-Identity

The final component that often becomes increasingly prevalent in your twenties and thirties is the journey of becoming aware of your own unique self-identity. You are likely to start focusing on your individual uniqueness as a result of pressure from others to "figure your life out" and "decide what you're going to do with your life."

It is likely you will learn a lot about yourself when put in a position to make a choice. At this stage of life, you are making so many critical life choices, such as:

- What type of job do I want?

- Who will I surround myself with?
- Where will I live?
- Should I change jobs?
- What should I buy—a house? A vehicle? IRAs?

Personal values are typically an internal metric that influence the way we live and operate in the world. However, when making a choice, our thinking can often be made much more visible, and our values are manifested out into the world, whether we realize it or not.

Additionally, we often tend to focus on personal growth and development in our twenties and thirties. Many people begin to see themselves in comparison to other people, which can often be a motivating factor to self-improve.

This internal understanding of who you are is the focus of this book. Without this, the pressure of everything happening in the world around you can cause you to doubt yourself. Doubt can limit you by negatively influencing the choices you make. Throughout this book, we will discuss how to focus on personal growth and development that allows you to maintain your natural uniqueness while also continuously improving to become the best version of yourself.

Doubt in the Wild

My twenties felt like chaos. My worst decade. I didn't know who I was or what I was doing... I was seeking, but not looking. Searching, but blind. I think back on my twenties as the most painful decade of my life. I attribute this to not knowing who I was or where I fit.

—Aaron D.

My Change and Transitions

While writing this book, I personally experienced a huge amount of change and transition. When I initially started to conceptualize this book, I was working in the field of public education. I served as a middle school math teacher for several years, an instructional coach for teachers, and then in more of a school administrator's role focusing on student discipline and developing a positive school culture and climate. Next I started to explore new opportunities, and currently I'm working as a full-time coach in a young company where I coach individuals through the writing and publishing process of their books.

While writing this book, I found myself diving into the process of purchasing my first home, moving my dog, Chip, and myself into a new location away from friends and family, and experiencing firsthand the new "adventures" of homeownership. I also found myself transitioning out of a long-term relationship and developing new friendships. Additionally, I became certified as a Myers-Briggs Practitioner and provided coaching opportunities to companies and individuals.

Not only did I get a new job, but I completely changed careers from public education into the business world. I found myself immersed in a company with an entrepreneurial spirit and more of a start-up vibe. This alone was a huge change from my experience working in public education. My location changed as I purchased my first home. My friendships and other relationships changed and developed. Needless to say, I've experienced my fair share of changes and transitions while writing this book.

Throughout all of this, I certainly received a lot of support from family and friends. However, there were many moments when the uncertainty of my future caused me to experience self-doubt. I was questioning myself, comparing myself to others, and feeling unsure about the choices I needed to make: "Is it the right time to buy a house, especially in a location that's new to me? What if I don't end up liking the place, but I'm stuck with the house, unable to sell? Maybe this is a bad move working at this startup because it's so young, it could fold? A career in public education is certainly more secure..."

I had many people question my decisions, especially in the choice to take a step back from public education and start a brand-new position that did not, at the surface, appear to be related to my previous experience or to the years and money I put in earning my education-related degrees: "Gary, why would you change careers when you've put so much time into teaching and schools? Don't you still have loans you're paying off for that master's degree in education?"

Although I found myself questioning and doubting my choices at times, this journey of self-discovery has been key in helping me navigate the many changes and transitions that I encountered while writing this book. My self-understanding has been key in embracing these choices and changes with an "adventure mindset" as opposed to allowing them to fuel self-doubt and fear. I found myself feeling much more confident in making a career change because I knew the change was better aligned with the way that I think and would allow me to live in my strengths. I was basking in the possibilities: "Now that I know I thrive in one-on-one conversations discussing the future, transitioning into a coaching role would be much more satisfying than having student discipline conversations."

In this book, I ultimately want to strengthen your understanding of who you are and what makes you unique. In turn, this will increase your sense of confidence as you too encounter changes, transitions, and important life decisions in this period of your life. Let's equip you with what you need to move from a space of self-doubt to, instead, being able to make the choice to live your best life.

Your Inner and Outer Worlds

So far, the majority of this introduction has focused on what I will call the "outer world." The outer world is inclusive of your job, all forms of relationships, and events in your life. The outer world includes where you are living, your interactions with others, and the act of making choices about educational experiences as well as career pathways.

As we grow older, the vast majority of people focus more and more on the outer world—of people, places, events, and things. When too much of our focus is on the outer world, it often negatively impacts our inner world, which we will explore in the next two chapters.

> **Outer World**
> *Your surroundings. This includes other people, places, events, and things in your life.*

In contrast, each of us also has access to our inner world. Just like it sounds, this is what's going on inside of you. This is the way you think, feel, process, and operate internally. Every single person has an entirely unique internal process, and we will explore how to learn about the unique wiring of your inner world later in this book.

Inner World
Your internal uniqueness. This includes your unique way of thinking, feeling, processing, and making decisions.

Stop & Think

1. What changes and transitions have you recently encountered in your life?

2. Who do you spend most of your time around? What are the relationships that are most important to you? Are your answers the same or different to these two questions?

3. How do you choose what path to take when faced with a critical decision? Are there particular values that influence your choices?

A Story of Choice

Enjoy the following thoughts from Jessica W. (age 30), sharing when she experiences doubt and when she's at her best.

Doubt in the Wild

I remember experiencing doubt when I was making the decision to move across the country—from Michigan to California. I had to decide if I wanted to stay near my family or pursue a brand-new opportunity. I know that when I'm feeling stagnant, I often experience doubt and develop a desire for change. I struggle with uncertainty in what new options would be the most fulfilling.

Once I feel conviction toward a decision, it's easy for me to run with it and make it happen. But getting to that point often includes agonizing uncertainty and lack of clarity, inducing lack of action and "staying stuck" in less-fulfilling situations. This happens in all areas of life: jobs, hobbies, love, friendships, and location. I can't seem to fully love where I am, as I haven't figured out the things that make me truly happy.

Discover You at Your Best

I am at my best when I am experiencing joy and truly experiencing life. This tends to look like being with loved ones and focusing my attention toward the present moment. I am happiest when I am with people I care about, exploring, adventuring, or just doing the mundane. I am at my best when I don't let doubt overshadow the great. The weight of doubt is not good for my mental health and causes me to feel withdrawn, which is the opposite of what makes me feel my best. When I am at my best, I have clarity of mind, I notice the small beautiful details in the world around me (like the birds chirping and the sound of waves crashing). I can dream about life, eagerly set goals. I am more creative and happy and want to contagiously spread that joyous feeling to others.

Reflections from Gary

Let's face it, your twenties and thirties are hard! There are so many changes and transitions that are constantly occurring in this time of your life. But on the flip side, notice the shift here. When Jessica is able to shift her mindset to the greatness in life, she is able to see the beauty in the world around her and envision a better future. This is the main objective of this book: to support you in moving from doubt to a great sense of conviction in the choices you make when facing change in your life. Let's continue to move from doubt to adventure by focusing on the great and beautiful things in life!

CHAPTER 3

Doubt

When faced with so many changes, transitions, and important life decisions, it is very likely that you've experienced a feeling of self-doubt before. Uncertainty influences you to question whether or not you're making the "right" choices.

When in the midst of making a decision, it's very possible that you become frozen in fear. Fear can stem from a wide variety of sources, and fear doesn't always have to be a negative thing. However, fear can prevent you from taking risks that can grow, stretch, and develop you into a better version of yourself.

Wavering self-esteem and self-confidence can prevent you from moving forward in the best possible way. Having a firm understanding of who you are, what makes you unique, and what you really want and need is essential when making decisions in times of change and transition. Making these decisions can liberate you because they'll allow you to feel like you're operating out of your natural strengths.

Often doubt, fear, or a low sense of self-esteem and self-confidence are rooted in various limiting beliefs. These beliefs have a tendency to constrain your mind from seeing your full potential. A limiting belief, just like it sounds, limits or prevents you from being the best version of who you are as an individual. Limiting beliefs are often rooted in thinking that you are lacking something.

Cause of Doubt

Just like we discussed in the previous chapter, every single person has access to their inner and outer worlds. A lot of time, doubt starts to form as a result of people, places, things, or events in the outer world.

Comparison

One common source of doubt is a result of comparing yourself to other people. You are likely looking at your day-to-day life in comparison to other people's—whether it is that of friends, family members, or coworkers.

Especially now in the world of social media, we compare the individual lives that we are living to those of other people we know. It is not uncommon for people to post the highlights of their life on various social media platforms. Posting pictures of milestone events—moving away, graduating college, getting married, having a baby, or buying a first home—seems to be common occurrences in the social media accounts of twenty- and thirty-year olds.

This results in you looking at your day-to-day life in comparison to those milestone events. Although there's nothing wrong with celebrating others' major milestones and wins, it can be incredibly unhealthy to "measure up" your own life against the lives of other people. Additionally, people rarely post about the struggles they experience and the monotony of their daily lives.

We are often comparing ourselves to others for a variety of reasons: admiration, competition, or jealousy. Let's explore these three reasons simply to get you thinking about the possible reasons behind why you may be comparing your life to the lives of other people. In examining these three reasons, you should recognize that comparing yourself is incredibly unhelpful.

> **Doubt in the Wild**
> *When I think about the future, it's such an unknown. Sometimes I find myself doubting that I can achieve all I want to achieve—in relationships, career goals, personal goals, etc. Typically it's because of comparison with other people: how does my life measure up with someone else's life according to their age, experience, and/or accomplishments?*
> —Ryan C. (age 29)

Admiration

Sometimes we find ourselves comparing our lives to other people's because we admire them. When we approve of their choices, we may want to emulate them. In this form, the comparison is rooted in a positive state of being because we see the best in someone else. However, at the end of the day, you're still comparing yourself to another person who isn't you!

This can be a dangerous choice because you're using an external measurement, something in your outer world, to determine the worth and value of your life. Additionally, we are often seeing the "best" aspects of the lives of others. This means we are disproportionately experiencing our own chaotic and busy lives, often sparking self-doubt. Even if you feel as though you're comparing your life to another person's from a healthy space of admiration, it is possible that you're limiting your own potential as a result of your focus on a single aspect or two in the outer world of another person.

Competition

Other times, you may compare yourself to the lives of others from a drive of competition. Some people are naturally competitive human beings. Maybe you can't stand the thought of another person outperforming you. Or maybe it's that you simply want to be the best. Although a dose of competition can be healthy at times to motivate you to become better, it may again become unhealthy.

As an educator, I saw this all the time in my students. Students were constantly looking at their grades and comparing them to others from a place of competition. In my advanced classes, students were constantly competing to be the top of their class. I also see this in the business world. We are surrounded by scoreboards in the outer world forcing us to see how we measure up against others. Young professionals are often looking to see how they're doing in sales, who is bringing in the most revenue, ultimately seeking to be at the top, no matter what metrics are being used.

The focus on the outer world of other people in the context of motivation might drive you to do things faster or better than other people. It is important to note that every person is unique and the act of comparing your life to the lives of others in order to be the best will not free you to be the best version of yourself as a human being. Instead, it will tether you to self-doubt as a result of comparing yourself to the outer world, rather than your own potential found in your inner world.

Jealousy

Sometimes, we are jealous of other people in our lives. When people accomplish things, it's possible that we begin to envy where they are at, the choices they've made, or the things that they have done. There are some characteristics that appear to be similar between a competitive drive to be the best and jealousy.

It is common that jealousy is a result of wanting something that someone else has. Instead of being genuinely happy for that person and their accomplishment, we often feel overwhelmed with a negative state of being because we so desperately want what that other person has. Maybe it's the car you've always wanted, the house that you've been searching for, or the relationship that you've always envisioned for your life. We are constantly surrounded by messages from the media and marketing professionals encouraging us to seek things that the world has placed value on.

We would typically want to be happy about things or accomplishments of others so that we can celebrate the highlights they've experienced. However, internally, we feel a deep draw to have those things, and jealousy is sparked into our lives.

This form of comparison can be incredibly dangerous for several reasons. First, it can be detrimental to interpersonal relationships in your life. Instead of being genuinely happy for other people, you begin to develop negativity towards the things that they've accomplished. Second, jealousy can freeze you from moving forward in your own life. Instead of having a healthy balance, you are so focused on the external accomplishments of people in your outer world, you are suddenly no longer able to see your own worth and value. Finally, envy and jealousy can be incredibly destructive. Jealousy can cause you to want something so bad that you're willing to destroy whatever is in your path to achieve that sense of success or bring others down in the process.

Uncertainty

In addition to doubt being caused by comparing ourselves to other people, we can often begin to experience doubt when things are uncertain in our outer world. For example, when we are facing unknowns and variables outside of our control. Let's look at these two in more detail.

Unknowns

When we look to the future of our own lives, uncertainty can be caused simply by the fact that we cannot anticipate everything that will happen. Looking ahead, there will always be things that we do not yet know about our future.

The unknowns that exist in our lives can cause us to experience a sense of uncertainty. When we are uncertain due to not knowing what will occur in the future, we can begin to experience doubt. This doubt sparked by the unknown will likely freeze you from living your best life.

Doubt in the Wild
I remember the time I sold all my possessions and moved to Canada for two years. Getting on that plane, I was filled with self-doubt because I had no idea what lay on the other side... the unknown is scary. That self-doubt I carried with me all the way to Canada led me to make a few bad decisions... like booking a place to stay in Vancouver sight-unseen... landing me in a dodgy place all alone. Thankfully, I also got myself out of that situation and into a safer area.
—Lise C.

Variables Outside of Control

Uncertainty, one of the primary causes of doubt, can also play out as a result of obsessing over variables that are outside of your control. We often let our minds obsess over all of the things that could happen or could go wrong. When we do this, energy from our inner world is being exhausted on things in our outer world that we have zero control over. Our minds are simply spiraling out of control over things that may or may not even happen.

So, What Is Doubt?

At this point, I've used the word "doubt" many times . . . but what exactly causes doubt? If you focus too much of your attention on the outer world, you will often lose sight of the uniqueness that exists in your inner world. This often results in comparing yourself to the lives of others.

Alternatively, if you focus too much of your attention on your inner world, you will often lose sight of taking action in the outer world. This will often result in the inner feeling of overwhelm and result in you feeling a sense of uncertainty.

The key here is to maintain balance between your inner and outer worlds. A lack of balance between your inner and outer world is the cause of doubt.

Doubt
A lack of balance between your inner and outer worlds.

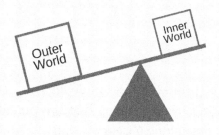

Self-Doubt or Your Best Life?

Let's face it, we can't each control all of the variables in our lives or predict with certainty how our futures will play out. There will always be things that are out of our control and it's up to us as individuals how we will respond to this fact. So, how in the world do we maintain balance to overcome doubt?

In the illustration above, the fulcrum (also known as the pivot point . . . this is what you get when you have a former teacher writing this book!) is the key to maintaining balance. If you are going to maintain balance, you must make a choice.

You have a choice to how you will respond to uncertainty. I see two clear paths you can choose. The first path is to operate out of a place of doubt. This will cause you to second guess everything you are thinking, feeling, and experiencing since you can't anticipate what is going to happen next. Doubt can restrict your ability to live your best life. It often results in monotony and a life of status quo. Alternatively, the second path is to make the choice to view your life with a lens of adventure.

You cannot always influence the things in your outer world. There will always be things in your life that are out of your control. However, you can choose how you interpret the outer world of your life.

There's a story running through your mind every single day. You can influence this narrative by examining the script within yourself. This internal script can be rooted in a (1) negative interpretation of doubt or (2) a positive and exciting interpretation of adventure. By choosing adventure over doubt, you will be able to gain balance between the many changes occurring in your outer world and the uniqueness that exists in your inner world.

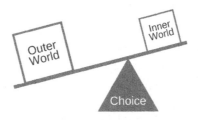

We will continue to explore how doubt vs. adventure can become a choice that you make in your life. It's a choice that can either give you (1) a perspective that limits you or (2) a perspective that gives you limitless possibilities in how you live out your life. Ultimately, the choice is yours. But the big question is this: if you have the power to end all doubt by making a choice to view life as an adventure, will you commit?

Result of Doubt in Our Inner World

Changes in jobs, relationships, finances, health, environment, and other major life circumstances can cause us to feel like we are swimming in doubt. When we focus on comparing our lives to the lives of others, we often begin experiencing self-doubt. Additionally, a focus on the uncertainty in our outer world can cause us to spiral out of control in our own minds. The reality is, doubt is caused by your outer world but has a ton of limiting power in your inner world.

Questioning

In your inner world, doubt can cause you to question yourself. Have you ever found yourself asking, "Am I enough? What's my worth? What's my value in the world?"

> **Doubt in the Wild**
> *I experienced doubt when I experienced my first post-grad failure in South Carolina. Less than three months into my move, the company I originally made the move for had financial issues and ultimately collapsed. Taking the risk to come to South Carolina and having a certain vision of how it would pan out, then to have that all be taken away REALLY made me doubt myself. I questioned my judgment, decision-making, willingness to take future risks, and also questioned what I wanted to do next.*
>
> *—Ryan M. (age 26)*

By asking yourself these questions from a perspective of doubt, it's likely that you will answer these questions from a very negative perspective. It's likely that instead of knowing that you are enough and that you have a unique purpose (more to come on all of this later), you'll question if you have anything you can contribute to the world.

Lack of Motivation

Have you ever had huge ambitions for your day, but then you were nearly stuck in your bed? Doubt can cause you to experience a lack of motivation. Those days that you just don't want to leave your house. Those days you just can't seem to tackle anything on your to-do list. Those days you can't find the motivation to interact with other people. Those days that you just can't seem to accomplish anything you originally thought you'd set out to do and complete.

Let me be clear, a lack of motivation is not exclusively caused by doubt. However, doubt can certainly cause you to experience a lack of motivation that freezes you from accomplishing things you want to do and thought you could do.

Lack of Fulfillment

Have you ever experienced a feeling like you were just moving through life, just simply going through the motions? The feeling that your life is just status quo at best? Maybe this feeling specifically stems from a lack of doing something that you feel serves or impacts other people in a significant way. It's not uncommon for doubt to cause a lack of fulfillment in your life.

> **Doubt in the Wild**
>
> *After I returned home from serving as a missionary in Kenya, I went back to working as a server again and I really questioned myself and my purpose! I wanted to do something worthwhile for the good of others and felt uncertain as to how and what to do. I went from feeling extremely passionate, proud, and excited about the work I was doing, to working a "meaningless" job. I really doubted myself and what I was supposed to be doing. What was my purpose now and who was I?*
>
> *—Rachel P. (age 27)*

Inner doubt limits the opportunity for adventure. We become victims of doubt instead of champions of our own adventures. Doubt makes us feel like we don't have a purpose and restricts us from finding adventure no matter the opportunities present in the current reality of our lives.

Lack of Confidence

Have you ever felt as though you just weren't good enough for something? Maybe it was a job that you'd love to apply for, an advanced program of study, or maybe an entire career path? Doubt can cause you to have crippling self-confidence that can stifle you from pursuing things in your life that you truly want.

Negative Self-Talk and Self-Criticism

Have you ever caught your mind spiraling out of control with negative thoughts about who you are as a human being? Have you noticed that you are often your biggest critic, picking apart every little action you've taken? Doubt also causes us to participate in negative self-talk and self-criticism.

The voice that whenever you try something new, it says no. Or the voice that when you make a mistake, says, "I told you so."

Inability to Make Decisions

At this point, it's evident that your twenties and thirties is a time full of change and transition. These changes and transitions often cause you to be at a fork in the road that requires you to make a choice. Instead of being able to clearly pick a path, have you ever caught yourself just standing at the fork in the road, not being able to make the decision at all? Maybe you're stuck overanalyzing the options? Maybe it's related to one of the previously mentioned points, such as a lack of confidence or just questioning every aspect of your life?

> **Doubt in the Wild**
> *When I found myself getting hired into my current job, I was by far the youngest employee on staff. I started experiencing doubt around my ability to lead others who were older and more experienced than I was in my job. Being comparatively young to others who I work with, while also being blessed to be in a position to lead, I felt a level of insecurity in my abilities to execute on that.*
> —*Pedro M. (age 20)*

Unfortunately, doubt can cause you to be frozen or unable to make decisions. This can result in you not moving forward confidently in a way that allows you to live your best life.

Disclaimer

By no means am I making the argument that you must stop doubting yourself in all areas of your life. Doubt, in a healthy dose, can cause us to recognize areas of our lives that we can become better. Doubt can cause us to grow, improve, and learn new things. When we experience self-doubt, it paints a picture of the line between comfort and adventure. All of this can be viewed as a positive result of doubt.

However, in this section, I am challenging the notion of doubt in an increased capacity that doesn't serve as a catalyst for growth, but rather paralyzes you from living your best life.

How to Stop Doubting Yourself

At this point, it is clear that doubt can be a force that limits you from taking action with confidence. In a period of your life like your twenties or thirties when there are so many changes and transitions occurring, doubt can truly limit your ability to live your best life. Let's dive into what exactly you can do about doubt.

Physiological Response

To get started, I would challenge you to stop and think about doubt in your life. Think about your answers to the following questions:

- What aspects of your life do you tend to experience self-doubt?

- How exactly do you know when you're experiencing doubt?

- What does your unique expression of doubt look like?

- What does it feel like?

- What does it sound like in your mind?

- How does doubt cause you to interact differently with others?

These questions, if answered honestly, will allow you to understand how doubt is playing out in your life decisions. The fascinating thing is that our bodies can often react in a similar way when we are experiencing different feelings. It is not uncommon for your heart rate to increase, you begin breathing rapidly, and you might even start sweating in response to a number of circumstances. These are all physiological signs of the feelings of excitement and adventure, as well as of fear, anxiety (not to be confused with anxiety disorder), and nervousness.

So if our body signals us in the same way for all of these feelings, though some are positive and some negative, what's the difference? The big difference between these feelings is how we internalize what's happening in the outer world. We can internalize things positively or negatively, and we can often influence these feelings through how we choose to understand the world around us.

It's clear that doubt is caused by factors in your outer world. It's a powerful force that causes you to negatively internalize things that are happening outside of your own mind, body, and soul. So here's the first step when encountering doubt (that is sparked by the outer world): you need to take a journey inside to your inner world.

Let's get even more specific. What if there was a way to change the way that you're perceiving "doubt" in the first place? I mentioned above that you have a choice when you begin to encounter doubt.

You can make the choice to call it "doubt," or to call it "an adventure." This is where we will begin to find the solution to doubt. But first, I want you to see how our bodies naturally signal to us that something in our life is out of balance.

Stop & Think

<u>Reminder:</u> These are not just questions for you to passively read. I encourage you to make your answers concrete by writing them down at the end of each chapter! If you haven't already, download the free digital workbook using the link at the beginning of this book in order to make the most out of your experience with this book!

1. When is a specific moment that you remember experiencing self-doubt?

2. What is the result of doubt in your inner world?

3. Which path will you choose to take, doubt or adventure?

    - ❏ If you decide to choose doubt, you are choosing to live a life that's lacking balance between your inner and outer worlds. If that's what you're looking for, go ahead and stop reading this book. The choice is yours!

    - ❏ If you decide to choose adventure, you are choosing to seek balance between your inner and outer worlds. We will continue to embark down this journey together through this book. The choice is yours!

A Story of Choice

Enjoy the following reflections from Melanie W. (age 26), sharing when she experiences doubt and when she's at her best in everything from her teaching career to her relationships.

Doubt in the Wild

I'm actually experiencing self-doubt right now. I am trying to decide whether or not to continue teaching or to try to switch to a different career, as well as decide whether or not to take the next step by moving across the country for my boyfriend, which also implies a lot about the status of our relationship—is he the one? I feel like I have no clarity! It's hard to make decisions based on others' and society's expectations as well.

Adventure at Your Best

When I'm at my best, I have clarity of mind and a calm energy—I'd probably call it a "buzz." I am able to engage with others authentically and adapt easily when things don't go as planned. I think about my good days as a teacher: I am able to keep an urgent, purposeful pace in the classroom with laughter, connection, and on-the-fly teachable moments interspersed throughout.

Reflections from Gary

Melanie is facing some major life decisions and, as a result of doubt, is experiencing internal questioning and a lack clarity just like we discussed in this chapter. It also sounds like she may be comparing or measuring up her decisions to what the world is expecting from her. On the flip side, at her best she is able to interact in a way that feels immediately clear and authentic. Her classroom is a better place when Melanie is able to maintain a healthy balance and overcome doubt. Let's continue to create laughter and connection by overcoming doubt together.

CHAPTER 4

Stress

Let's face it, stress is inevitable. Our bodies have an incredible way of handling life when things aren't going the right way. In this chapter, we are going to explore the topic of stress.

I am defining stress as a signal that there is a lack of balance in our lives. Stress can function like a siren alerting us that something is not right. This siren can be a signal to help us see when doubt may begin creeping into our minds. We all experience stress, but the way that it manifests will be different for each person.

Stress, Stressors, and Strain

The overall idea here is the term stress. One critical distinction when discussing the topic of stress is to identify the difference between stressors and strain.

Stressors

Knowing what stressors are is important because of how we use this language daily. How many times have you, or someone you know, said something along the lines of "I'm so stressed out!" By creating a separation in this language, you can hopefully begin to identify what your stressors are that are causing you to experience stress.

When we are examining the topic of stress, stressors are the things that cause us to experience stress. Stressors are things in our outer world that are causing us to experience stress.

Some stressors are "bigger picture" things happening in our lives that stick with us for awhile. For example, being a caretaker for a loved one for years, determining what career path to follow, or determining where and when to purchase your first home. Other stressors appear to be "smaller" in scale, but can still cause us to experience stress. For example, balancing your workload due to an upcoming deadline, deciding how to spend your time on a particular weekend, or determining how to respond to a small interpersonal dispute with a family member or friend. By identifying the stressors, or the specific things that are causing you stress, you can begin to recognize these patterns and start to gain control over how these stressors influence you.

What are the stressors that are causing you the most stress in your life? Think about your...

- Job—coworkers, tasks, deadlines, projects, etc.

- Relationships—friendships, romantic relationships, pressures of marriage, etc.

- Family—parents, siblings, grandparents, etc.

- Living Arrangement—moving, apartment living, home ownership, etc.

- Education—training, higher education, assignments, decision-making, etc.

Doubt in the Wild
I experienced a ton of doubt when dropping out of school to try and start my business. My business was failing, I moved across the country, and the only girl I would say I was in love with just happened to be the first girl that ever dumped me. During this time, most of my doubt was around whether or not I made the right decision to drop out and whether or not I would be successful as an entrepreneur... especially as pretty much everyone in my life (besides my immediate family) thought I was making a bad decision.
—*Chandler B. (age 25)*

Strain

If stressors are the factors in our outer world that cause stress, strain is what we are experiencing in our mind and body as a result of the stressors.

The stressors in your life can potentially have an extremely negative effect on your body. One of the most powerful things about recognizing how stressors are causing strain in your body is that you can become aware of when your stress levels are approaching an unhealthy level. This will hopefully allow you to intervene earlier before the stressors cause you too much strain and the stress becomes unmanageable.

How do you typically know that your stress is negatively impacting you? Note that the strain is usually a physiological response in your body, but you may also be able to recognize that your stress levels are becoming unhealthy due to behavioral changes:

- Physical Pain—headaches, body aches, etc.
- Abdominal/Stomach Issues
- Quality of Sleep
- Productivity Levels
- Inability to Focus

Behavioral Changes Due to Stress

As noted above, stress can cause physical changes to your body (strains) that can impact your overall health and wellbeing. However, stress can also change the way that you think, act, and behave. In this section, we will explore two common ways that unhealthy levels of stress can impact your behavior.

Your Best Self Exaggerated

Imagine the very best version of yourself. Whatever qualities that pop in your mind, these are likely some of your strengths. These are the qualities that other people will often use to describe you.

However, when high levels of stress are introduced into your life, it is possible that these best qualities of who you are as a human being quickly become overly exaggerated. These strengths or aspects of what makes you unique may quickly become overbearing and begin to become "immature" in the way that they are lived out.

For example, maybe you are someone who is well-known for being well-thought-out, a planner, someone who brings structure to other people and situations. If you're encountering high levels of stress, it's likely that you become overly fixated on scheduling your life or the lives of others, likely in attempt to gain control of everything you possibly can though you may not realize it.

Or maybe you are someone who takes pride in the relationships that you build with others, you are great at creating welcoming environments, building morale, and you love helping and serving others. If this is you, when experiencing too much stress, you will likely begin to completely disregard your own needs and become fixated on meeting the needs of other people.

These are just two examples of how your best qualities could become overly exaggerated when you are experiencing high levels of stress. In this state, you are no longer using those best qualities of yourself to do what you do best. These qualities begin to enter an unhealthy state and, therefore, begin to show up in a negative or immature way.

Your Unnatural State of Being

As we dive deeper into this book, we will spend more time together discussing how you can begin to understand your natural uniqueness as a human being. However, it should be noted that unhealthy levels of stress can cause you to operate out of your unnatural state.

This is important to recognize now, before we begin exploring what makes you unique, simply because the behaviors you are demonstrating might not be your "best self" if your levels of stress are too high.

> **Doubt in the Wild**
> *I experience self-doubt when sharing personal experiences in a group setting with people whom I just meet or whom I sense are judging me. The aftermath is the hardest part because I start to wonder what I should not have shared. Basically, I start ruminating, replaying what I shared over and over again in my mind and chastising myself for it (whether rightly or wrongly). This whole situation sucks because you want to be real with people when prompted, but you also want to protect yourself.*
> —Jessica L. (age 23)

For example, if you are someone who is generally quite sociable, it is possible that in times of high stress you may isolate yourself from others.

If you are someone who is generally quite easy-going and adaptable, in times of high stress you may try to gain control of absolutely everything you can in your life.

If you are someone who is grounded and thrives at being responsible, dependable, and loyal, in times of high stress you may experience your mind spiraling out of control, imagining absolutely everything that could go wrong.

If you are someone who thrives at coming up with ideas and dreaming up possibilities for the future, it is very possible that in times of extreme stress you may become overindulgent in things you don't usually struggle with, such as television, food, or shopping.

These are just a few examples to explore how when you are extremely stressed, you may quickly "flip" to operate out of a space that is counter to what you would generally consider to be the best version of yourself.

Maintaining Balance

As we continue into this book, you will notice a major part of our discussion is how to maintain balance with your particular natural state of being. The awareness of your individual uniqueness, specifically the uniqueness of your inner world, will allow for you to keep this natural part of your identity the focus, even during times of stress.

The Power of Perception

One of the most powerful forces to overcome the unhealthy strains of stressors in your life is simply your perception. We have a choice to make whenever we encounter stress in our outer world, and it's really quite simple. We have the choice to decide how to internalize and process the stressful factors in our lives.

Your individual perception of events in the outer world can greatly impact the strain that those stressors have on your life. If you choose the point of view that things in your life are incredibly stressful and you allow them to limit you from moving forward, it's likely these stressors will have a greater impact on your health, wellbeing, and general self-conception. When you view aspects of your outer world as being more stressful than they really are, you will negatively impact your total sense of who you are. It can begin to limit what you believe you can achieve, causing other things to be impossible, when they are things you can easily manage.

However, if you choose to recognize the things in your life that may be causing you stress, but you decide not to allow them to control your mind or limit your actions, you will likely see less of an impact on your health, wellbeing, and self-conception as a person in this world. The series of choices in how you perceive your outer world can be powerful in shaping you to live your best life.

> **Doubt in the Wild**
> *Doubt was experienced during my first job. I had doubt in my ability to be able to find a new job, so it was keeping me at a job I hated. Once I overcame that doubt, I realized you should never stay at a job you hate, and I will carry this insight through my professional career.*
> —Michael S. (age 25)

One concrete tip to influence your perception is to think about the variables that are in your control. There's a term called "locus of control." This can be explored from both an internal (inner world) or external (outer world) point of view.

If your **locus of control** is focused on the **outer world**, you will likely blame other people and situations for everything going on for you in your life. Your focus is on the fact that you cannot control everything in your life. Although this is true, an external locus of control can cause you to get out of balance, and it encourages stress to have an even greater detrimental impact on your personal wellbeing.

In contrast, an **internal locus of control**, or a focus on your **inner world**, influences you to focus on the factors in your life that you truly have control over. Although you cannot control everything, there are certainly things in every situation that you have the power to influence or control. One consistent aspect of your life that you *always* have control over is how you perceive the outer world.

Even in the most chaotic and stressful situations, you have the power to influence your own personal perception of what's occurring in your life.

The interpretation of your outer world can influence the way you view your inner world. You have a choice in how you will view the world around you. Interpreting the world around you as uncontrollable and something you cannot influence at all will paralyze you and influence you to self-doubt. However, identifying the things that are within your locus of control and having a healthy interpretation of events in the outer world can put you on the path to choosing your best life.

Stop & Think

1. What are the primary stressors in your life?

2. When you experience stress, what evidence of strain have you experienced? What behavioral changes do you notice yourself exhibiting?

3. Concerning what aspects of your life do you tend towards having an external locus of control? Internal locus of control? How can shifting your focus towards the inner world help you to choose your best life?

A Story of Choice

Enjoy the following thoughts from Andrea Z. (age 25), sharing when she experiences doubt and when she's at her quirky best.

Doubt in the Wild

A few months after graduating college, I still couldn't find a job (in my field of study). I'd been applying for months and was really doubting myself when I wasn't even getting "rejection emails." I was second-guessing if I should continue to pursue jobs in my field or if I should take any job I could get. Mostly, everyone was saying, "Take any job you can get" or "Get your foot in the door." They were pretty much telling me to settle. I didn't want to settle just yet! So, there was a little bit of hope in my doubting. Also, NO ONE giving me this advice was in my "field," so they didn't understand. But, it helped when half of my graduating class was going through the same thing.

Discover You at Your Best

I am at my best when I'm stress-free. I'm creative, but sometimes I need someone to give me a challenge or give me restraints; otherwise I will overthink and doubt everything! I'm definitely at my best when I'm not afraid to be myself. I was in an interview, and I felt like I was 100% quirky me. I felt great. I felt like I was connecting with people, asking them questions, and really I felt like friends with each and every one of them. (Even if they didn't find this charming, I left the interview feeling like I laid it all out on the table.) When I'm care-free, I'm definitely at my best.

Reflections from Gary

What Andrea is expressing here is not uncommon for recent college graduates. She knew what type of job she wanted to take and didn't want to settle. However, this sparked some doubt as she was going months without finding a job. Just as we discussed in this chapter, Andrea had to create a balance between her inner and outer world to prevent herself from getting stagnant. On the flip side, when she is at her best, she's able to connect with people in an authentic and meaningful way. It sounds like a healthy dose of creative constraints liberates Andrea to work within the framework she's given, and what's impressive is that she knows this about herself; it's part of her individual uniqueness. Let's take Andrea's cue and continue to embark on an adventure of creativity by viewing constraints with a positive lens instead of a feeling of restriction!

CHAPTER 5

Your Individual Uniqueness

One of the most fascinating things about human beings is that every single human being is unique. No two humans are the same —even identical twins. Right down to the details of your fingerprints, every individual has aspects that make them unique.

Inner vs. Outer World

So at this point, one of the most common questions that people grapple with is "What makes people unique?" Is it nature or nurture? Are there innate differences in people from the moment we are born? Or is it the culmination of our worldly experiences that causes us to be unique?

To me, the answer is very clear: it's both. There is evidence to show that human beings have inborn preferences that cause them to be unique from the very moment they are born. However, these preferences are grown and shaped by the unique life experiences that every single person has as they grow up.

This points to the fact that uniqueness is shaped by your inner and outer worlds, or nature and nurture respectively. We started this book by first looking at the changes and transitions that you are encountering or will likely encounter in your life; these are factors in your outer world. Next, we discussed the impact of doubt and stress in both your inner and outer worlds. Now, we continue by examining specifically what makes you unique in your inner world.

Wiring of Your Mind

The way you think, act, and behave are all influenced by the unique way that your mind is wired. The wiring of your mind (your inner world) influences the way that you interact with other people, events, or situations (your outer world).

By gaining a better understanding of your inner world, you'll not only be able to see patterns in your previous behavior, but you'll likely be able to anticipate how you might respond in the future. As discussed previously, doubt is caused by factors in the outer world (stressors) and results in the signal of stress (strain). In turn, by gaining a clearer understanding of your inner world, you'll be able to see the power that's within you to make a series of choices that will allow you to live your best life.

Truly understanding your own uniqueness will allow you to see your inner strength. Instead of constantly measuring yourself up against the rest of the world (which is a primary source of doubt), you'll be able to compare yourself against your own greatness.

Let me be crystal clear here: a better understanding of what makes you unique allows you to unlock the greatest measuring stick of all: your own potential. It's finally time to stop comparing yourself to others, and it's time to start using your own unique potential to measure the trajectory of your life.

How Do I Begin to Understand My Inner World?

Every single person is unique, and because of this, it can be challenging to understand your inner world. This is especially true because each person's "inner world" is usually hidden from others. Unless you're explicitly talking about your process of doing something, it is incredibly rare that we understand what's happening in another person's mind.

There are a variety of personality metrics, tools, and assessments that have helped many people begin to understand their own uniqueness. In this book, we will dive into one of these tools to begin building a common language about your unique inner world.

In this book, we will use the framework originally conceptualized by the celebrated Swiss psychoanalyst, Carl Jung, that was later developed into the Myers-Briggs Type Indicator (MBTI), a tool that helps people understand their natural preferences. The tool is designed to help people identify the patterns of behavior originally conceived by Carl Jung.

A critical part of Jung's original theory presented in his book *Psychological Types* is that people have inborn or innate preferences. Although your environment can influence you, Jung believed that people each have unique *preferences* in every aspect of their lives.

Although you are not always going to solely operate out of your natural preferences, you still have a preference. Our bodies naturally have preferences that we primarily operate out of. From a very young age, we naturally prefer one hand over the other. We also have preferences for types of food that we like or experiences we enjoy.

We also have internal preferences that make up the individual uniqueness within each of us. Your individual uniqueness results in you having innate preferences in the way that you think, act, and behave in our world. In this book, we will continue to look at some of these preferences that you have that make up your unique personality.

Jung's original theory and framework was later expanded upon by Isabel Myers and Katharine Briggs who began developing a practical tool for people to self-reflect and increase their self-understanding. According to the Myers & Briggs Foundation, this mother and daughter team had a goal to "enhance harmony and productivity in diverse groups." In order to help people apply and understand the framework of Carl Jung, they developed a questionnaire that became the Myers-Briggs Type Indicator (MBTI).

The work of Myers and Briggs has influenced the way that I see myself (my inner world) and the way that I interact with others (in the outer world). I first encountered this instrument when I was in middle school, and it has revolutionized the way that I operate. In this book, I want to share this tool with you in a way that's directly applicable to your life. I'm not aiming to get caught up in theoretical implications of personality, but instead to dive into a framework that will help you see your individual uniqueness and, in turn, the uniqueness of others. As a result, you'll be able to harness these findings to overcome self-doubt by making choices that embrace your natural preferences, instead of aiming to live to the expectations presented in your outer world.

Let's dive a little bit into how the indicator is structured.

Dichotomies

In the Myers-Briggs Type Indicator framework, there are a series of questions to help you identify your natural preferences in four critical areas. This framework will help you see your natural preferences in (1) your energy, (2) how you understand the world around you, (3) how you make decisions, and (4) your approach to structure in the outer world.

These four areas each have two different options, or preferences. The pairs of preferences are known as dichotomies. The instrument is designed to sort you into seeing your natural preference between the two options. The four dichotomies, with eight preferences in total, develops a framework of sixteen individual personality types.

A critical part of this framework is the concept of preferences. You have a preferred hand, but you are not limited to only using that hand. The same thing is true for your individual personality. This tool is structured to help you identify your natural preferences in four distinct dichotomies. Let's take a look at a high-level overview of each of the four dichotomies illustrated by the Myers-Briggs Type Indicator.

My challenge for you moving forward is to trust the framework and begin to realize that these differences in preference certainly exist between people. Our goal is to determine which option you most naturally prefer. Don't feel as though you're exclusively limited to one out of the two options in each dichotomy because every person has access to both of the preferences. Once you identify your natural preference, it will be easier for you to maintain a sense of balance. However, at the end of the day, one of the two options is typically more comfortable and requires less work for you to live out.

For the Critics, Skeptics, and Naysayers

Every tool has had its fair share of critics, skeptics, and naysayers. There have been plenty of people who have rejected the Myers-Briggs Type Indicator (MBTI) and the original concepts from Carl Jung. In my studies, I have found that many people who reject MBTI don't fully understand the intent behind the tool.

Psychologists

As an undergraduate student, I studied the field of psychology, and I quickly learned that many psychologists have rejected the Myers-Briggs Type Indicator. One common reason for this is that they generally prefer to measure "how much" of a trait exists within a person whereas this tool is simply designed to sort based on preferences. Many psychologists prefer to measure quantitatively how much of a trait exists in order to determine correlation between personality traits and other psychological measures. It is common practice for psychologists to view traits on a continuum, or to standardize results on a normative scale such as a standard bell curve to compare the results of one individual to the results of others.

Although it can be helpful to measure the degree to which a trait exists, that is not the goal in the MBTI assessment or many other personality-type tools. The goal in these indicators is simply to help sort out your natural preferences, not to measure quantitatively the extent that you exhibit a trait.

My challenge for you here is to clearly identify the goal that you are trying to achieve before selecting a tool. If your goal is to measure the degree to which a personality trait exists, tools such as the MBTI assessment will simply not be a good fit to make your end goal become a reality.

I Don't Fit in a Box

You're absolutely right, you don't fit in a box. I always caution people as they dive into tools such as the Myers-Briggs Type Indicator to take the results with a grain of salt. There is certainly no way to split the world's population into sixteen perfect boxes. The whole point of this tool is to begin to identify natural preferences . . . not to identify who you are as a human being.

Most tools only aim to sort out certain patterns of behaviors. I have yet to come across a tool that accurately categorizes all forms of human behavior in one tool. Again, our goal here isn't to define who you are, but to simply identify patterns that are unique to you and your inner world, so you can begin seeing the power that you have within yourself.

My challenge for you here is to not allow results from these types of tools to limit you or to even accept them as the ultimate "truth." We simply are aiming to identify patterns in the way that you think, feel, and behave to begin to see what makes you unique.

My Results Are Always Different!

Maybe you've previously explored tools such as the MBTI assessment. With it being a common tool in most Fortune 500 companies and often used in educational settings, it's likely that you've encountered it before. I've repeatedly heard from people that every time they encounter the MBTI assessment, their results are different.

This is very possible, but it's important to consider why the results might vary. If the tool is given to you in a specific setting, you might take that setting or role into consideration when you are responding to items. For example, if you are responding to items with your job or workplace in mind, this could skew your results from identifying your natural preferences. You may instead identify how you *need* to operate at work to be "effective" in your job. This is why it's not effective to use the MBTI instrument for hiring purposes.

My challenge for you here is to consider your most natural state when using personality-type tools to get the most accurate results. Thinking about a specific role or position may significantly skew your results, or lead you to get different results each time you complete the assessment.

Big Picture

The goal in this book is to begin exploring patterns in your behavior by identifying your natural preferences. The goal is not to limit you or define who you are. The aim is for you to begin building language that will empower you to see what makes you unique, so you can use the uniqueness of your inner world to overcome doubt caused by your outer world.

Okay... So What's Next?

Over the next four chapters, we will explore each of the four dichotomies using information from Carl Jung's *Psychological Types*, which was expanded by Myers and Briggs into the Myers-Briggs Type Indicator. Although factual information from Jung, Myers, and Briggs is included in the next chapters, the thoughts and opinions are my own based off of coaching experiences in the past.

Stop & Think

1. How many different ways can you honestly complete the following statement in sixty seconds? Make a list. Ready, set, go! "I prefer _____."

2. Describe your current attitude towards the MBTI instrument.

3. When are you at your best?

A Story of Choice

Enjoy the following thoughts from Erin R. (age 38), sharing when she experiences doubt and when she's her natural loving self, embracing adventure!

Doubt in the Wild

I lived A LOT of my twenties, especially, believing that I was unlovable and/or unworthy of love. Naturally, this affected my relationships and my belief in myself. If someone DID say I was beautiful or say they loved me, I suspected an ulterior motive because I KNEW those things weren't true. Eventually, I believed I could be loved . . . but still believed myself to be very small and insignificant (this is still something I'm overcoming).

Discover You at Your Best

I'm at my best when I'm saying yes to "risks" and experiencing how limiting my life had been up until that "yes"—getting to experience the amazing things that can happen when I step into unknowns, regardless of my confidence, trusting that something good and beautiful (and at least learn-worthy) will come from it. When I'm impacting people and helping others . . . experiencing new things with deep relationships . . . I'm at my best!

Reflections from Gary

Erin's reflections make me think of so many people I've talked with over the years. The power of our inner thoughts can influence our ability to receive the best in the outer world. Notice how Erin, at her best, is able to completely shift her thoughts to view herself from a place of potential, just as we started to discuss in this chapter. In this book, let's continue to learn how to see the true and authentic qualities that exist in our inner world that make us each beautiful in our own way. This sense of understanding in our inner world will let us see our own beauty, so we can overcome moments when we might usually experience self-doubt.

CHAPTER 6

Your Energy

In this chapter we are going to take a look at how you most naturally direct and receive your energy, the first of the four dichotomies. Have you ever come home from a day of work and you just felt absolutely exhausted? Or maybe, on the other end of the spectrum, have you ever come home from work feeling energized and full of life?

We are going to take a look at what it is that might allow you to gain energy in your life, but also the things in your life that might have caused you to expend your energy. We are going to take a look at two different groups of people.

Gaining Energy from the Outer World

The first group of people are those that gain energy from being with other people. A good friend of mine, Lauren, has this ability to walk into any social setting and just beam with energy in every interaction she has with other people. She has this superpower to be able to connect with people in a way where she walks away feeling even more energized than before she began the social interaction.

People are naturally drawn to Lauren from the energy she sends off from the interactions she has with others. This energy is generally caused by the fact that Lauren is excited to be around other people, and she feels energized when she is surrounded by others.

Even in times when she is working independently on a task or a project, she often likes to be in the presence of other people, even if she isn't directly talking to them. Just being in the presence of other people allows her to complete the task more efficiently and with a greater sense of energy.

Lauren is more inclined to direct her energy to the outer world—to other people, events, or situations. I've noticed that people are often drawn to Lauren, but Lauren is also drawn to other people.

With her focus on the outer world, it's not uncommon for Lauren to process through things externally. I often notice Lauren will like to talk things out and have conversations about things she is experiencing personally or problems she is trying to solve. This practice of processing through things externally is an indication of her preference to direct her energy to the outer world.

Gaining Energy from the Inner World

In contrast to Lauren, another group of people is represented by my close friend Danielle. Danielle tends to spend more time by herself. Now let me be clear, this has zero indication of social skills or abilities or having a strong sense of emotional intelligence. Danielle is one of the most empathetic and loving human beings that I have ever met. Danielle is great at building social connections, but we are simply looking at the energy it takes to do this and where she prefers to direct her energy.

When I look at where Danielle most comfortably directs her energy, it is evident she directs her energy towards her inner world. Danielle often prefers to work independently and invests her time and energy towards her inner world.

By trade, Danielle is a designer and tends to thrive when she is able to direct her energy inward. She enjoys brainstorming new ideas and thinking about the world around her. Her focus is usually directed more towards her inner thoughts, feelings, experiences, memories, and her ideas.

A Healthy Balance in Preferences

Both Lauren and Danielle need a balance of spending time with other people and spending time alone. The goal here is simply to look at the most natural preference and where each person is most comfortable in how they direct and receive their energy. Lauren is more inclined to receive energy from the outer world whereas Danielle is more inclined to receive energy from her inner world.

Every single person has access to both their inner and outer worlds. But our goal here is to simply identify where you most naturally prefer to direct your energy. It's more likely that at the end of the day, Lauren would gain energy if she spent the day interacting with other people whereas Danielle is more likely to lose energy if she spent all day interacting with others.

However, from the opposite perspective, Lauren is more likely to feel drained or exhausted at the end of the day if she was alone. Danielle is more likely to have more energy at the end of the day if she spent her day alone with her energy focused inwards.

Extraversion vs. Introversion

The first dichotomy of preferences is where you focus your energy. There are two options, or preferences, and Jung's theory concludes that each person has a natural preference for one over the other.

Like Lauren, you might prefer to focus your energy on the outer world. Knowing this, this preference generally indicates a focus on people, events, and things—your surroundings. This preference is known as extraversion.

In contrast, other people (like Danielle) prefer to focus their energy on their inner world. Knowing this, this preference generally indicates a focus on inner thoughts, feelings, or memories. This preference is known as introversion.

Maybe you've heard of the terms extraversion and introversion previously. Some people have prior experiences with these terms, but I'd encourage you to focus on the meaning of the words provided here—examining where you are most inclined to direct and receive energy.

Remember, this dichotomy has nothing to do with measuring social skill or the degree to which a trait exists within you. This has nothing to do with you being outgoing, socially awkward, or being good with people.

It's likely that parts of both Lauren and Danielle resonate with you. Again, the goal isn't to isolate you and exclude you from accessing the other dimension. The goal is simply to help you sort out what your natural preference is between the two.

Where do you most naturally direct and receive your energy? Do you most naturally direct your energy towards your inner or outer world?

How Knowing This Can Overcome Doubt

In this book, it's our goal to help you understand your own individual uniqueness with the goal of overcoming doubt. By understanding your personal flow of energy, you can begin to understand one aspect of what makes you unique. Doubt is the lack of balance between your inner and outer worlds.

Before moving on . . . take a second to stop and think. Where do you most often direct and receive your energy?

If You Prefer Introversion . . .

Have you ever thought it was abnormal that after a long day of socializing, you just feel absolutely exhausted?

I have talked to so many people who thought they were crazy because of their natural preference for directing their energy towards the inner world. You might have caught yourself saying, "I never feel comfortable at large parties" or "Is it bad that sometimes I need to be alone and away from family and friends?" We live in a world that in many ways favors extraversion. It is often seen as being socially desirable to spend much of the time with other people.

Here's the beautiful thing about how you're wired: your thoughtful ability to reflect, think, and process through your inner world is a huge asset to our world. You have an incredible ability to think, feel, and process internally in a way that nearly half of our world's population will never fully understand.

It's likely you prefer to invest your energy in your inner world. By knowing that, you might spend more of your energy when you focus on the outer world. You can then make decisions about how to best protect your energy and maximize the natural inward orientation of your energy. Building in time that you are alone can sometimes help you to recharge and refuel by directing your energy towards your inner world.

I said it before, but it's so important I'm going to say it again. If you prefer introversion, you still have the ability to interact effectively with other people and direct your energy towards the outer world. You have, and always will have, access to both your inner and outer worlds.

You can apply this knowledge to help yourself overcome doubt by recognizing your natural preference for refueling and recharging your energy. If you naturally prefer introversion, it's essential that you honor this part of who you are by finding time to refuel. This will allow you to maintain a better balance between your inner and outer worlds, ultimately helping overcome doubt and embrace a sense of adventure.

If You Prefer Extraversion . . .

Have you ever thought it was abnormal that after a day of socializing, you feel energized and renewed?

If you prefer extraversion, it is likely that you naturally prefer to direct your energy outward to the outer world. This will likely cause you to be quick to take action and have a natural focus on the people, events, and occurrences that are in your outer world.

Here's the beautiful thing about how you're uniquely wired... your external focus on other people, events, and things is a huge asset to our world. You have an incredible ability to process the outer world in a way that's faster paced and that nearly half of our world's population will never fully understand.

It's likely you prefer to invest more of your energy in your outer world. By knowing that, you might expend more of your energy when you focus your energy in the inner world. You can make use of this information to choose how to best utilize your energy. Building in time that you are with other people or focused on external events can help you to recharge and refuel by directing your energy towards the outer world.

Again... if you prefer extraversion, it doesn't mean you will be able to spend all day every day with other people, focused on the outer world, and never feel exhausted. Every person needs a healthy balance of their inner and outer worlds. It's possible you still feel tired or exhausted at the end of the day working with other people—don't let that limit you.

Sometimes specific types of interactions can exhaust you faster than others. Beginning to pay attention to your energy levels throughout the day, at the end of the day, etc., can help you identify what it is that might exhaust you the most.

If you naturally prefer extraversion, it's essential that you honor this part of who you are by finding time to reconnect with others consistently. By embracing your natural preference, you will achieve greater balance between your inner and outer worlds, which will support you in embracing a life of adventure.

Overall

Knowing how you direct and receive your energy will allow you to be more intentional in how you use your energy in your day-to-day life.

The main goal here is for you to see the power of your natural preference when it comes to your energy. This is a starting point to overcome any doubt you might experience and to realize the way you direct and receive your energy is normal. Being aware of this can help you live a life with a greater degree of confidence.

As you encounter critical life choices, being aware of how you refuel and recharge can help you decide what will be healthy for you, so that you can diminish stressors. Remember, you are not limited by your natural preference, but this awareness can help you be proactive in living a balanced life. If you are experiencing the signal of stress in your life, consider if the stressor is related to your energy. This signal can help you make changes (internally or externally) that can help you push through possible causes of doubt.

Stop & Think

1. What do you do to direct your energy to your inner world?

2. What do you do to direct your energy to the outer world?

3. List three things that help you maintain balance between your inner world and the outer world.

A Story of Choice

Enjoy the following thoughts from Mary W. (age 27), sharing when she experiences doubt and when she's at her best by maintaining balance.

Doubt in the Wild

My career gives me the most doubt in my life. Am I on the right path? How can I advance? Do I like what I'm doing? How do I know if I am making the right choices? There are so many career options that I feel overwhelmed trying to decide what the right path is. I doubt every choice I make because I'm nervous about the outcome and don't want to be "stuck" in something.

Discover You at Your Best

I'm at my best when I am taking time for myself to balance out my outward obligations (work, family, friends, etc.). When I am able to replenish my needs, I perform better in all other areas of my life. For example, during my busy fall travel season at work, I take time every Sunday morning to watch something funny (SNL is my go-to). I like to make a nice breakfast, drink coffee, and laugh.

Reflections from Gary

In Mary's career, it sounds like she finds herself questioning the path she's on and the decisions she's making as a result of doubt. In order to remain at her best, Mary focuses on creating a sense of balance. After finishing this chapter on energy, you know the importance of maintaining balance between your inner and outer world. Based off of the examples provided by Mary, it's likely she naturally directs her energy to her inner world, which would indicate a preference of introversion. Mary is incredibly intentional about replenishing her needs, and this allows her to be at her best. No matter your natural preference, you can learn from Mary's ability to create balance between her work (outer world) and her personal needs (inner world). Let's continue to overcome doubt by creating a sense of balance in our energy!

CHAPTER 7

Understanding

Understanding

In this chapter, we are going to explore how you naturally understand the world around you and the types of information you prefer to receive, the second dichotomy. Have you noticed that you prefer when things are presented in a concrete and sequential way? Or maybe, you prefer things to be more theoretical in nature in order to draw your own conclusions?

We are going to dive into two different styles that will describe how you might prefer to take in information. It is likely that parts of both will resonate with you. That's completely normal. Again, our goal is to identify the natural preference between the two options listed below. One will be more natural, take less work, or be more comfortable for you ... that's your preference!

Be aware that this chapter is independent of the last chapter. You will have a preference in how your direct and receive energy, and this preference is separate from your preference of how you understand information.

Give Me the Details

The first group of people are those that prefer to take in information that is concrete, factual, and focused in on details and specifics. A good friend of mine, Brittany, has the ability to pick up on the small details that matter. She has an incredible memory and thrived in school when focused on memorizing the specifics. She understands the world around her by primarily using her five senses.

As a result of this, one of Brittany's greatest superpowers is being present in the current reality. When she is with others, she is great at staying in the present moment and engaging in the here and now. Additionally, she has the ability to pick up on the little details that matter—when many others don't always notice.

When Brittany presents a story to me, she has an incredible ability to walk me through step by step exactly what happened. I can easily hear a clear timeline that is sequential and well organized when listening to stories or information presented by her.

Give Me the Big Picture

The second group of people are those that prefer to take in information that is abstract, theoretical, and focused on relationships and patterns. A good friend of mine, Daniel, has the ability to quickly pick up on patterns and themes between things that other people might not even see a relationship between.

As a result of this, Daniel is incredibly strategic in his thinking, and his mind is often casting to envision future possibilities. He can often piece ambiguous pieces of information together to understand the bigger picture and to understand the meaning behind what's occurring in a series of events.

When Daniel presents a story to me, he will often lead with the highlights and focus most of his time and energy on the big idea or the meaning behind what happened. I don't always know the specifics behind what happened but will be crystal clear on the big idea or what a particular event means to him or to others. He will often connect various ideas together that may seem like they are not sequentially aligned in a timeline, but connect through a broader theme.

Sensing vs. Intuition

In the original framework constructed by Carl Jung, this dichotomy identifies how you prefer to understand or take in information. There are two options, or preferences, in this particular framework. Remember, you will use both every single day. But one of the two options is likely more comfortable and what you tend to prefer.

Some people prefer to take in information that is concrete, factual, black and white, or present in the here and now. This typically means that people who prefer this type of information will focus on presenting their ideas sequentially and with a focus on the details. This preference is known as sensing.

Some people prefer to take in information that is abstract, theoretical, or focused on the bigger picture. This will result in ideas being presented thematically or by focusing on the underlying meaning. This preference is known as intuition.

Remember, both of these preferences are essential to our world, and you will use both every single day. However, one of these preferences is what is most natural or comfortable for you. Neither preference is better than the other.

They both have an incredible amount of value, and I would challenge you to see the beauty in your natural preference. You are wired uniquely and knowing how you prefer to take in and receive information will help you develop a framework for how you see and interpret the world around you.

Dominant Preference

Most of the four dichotomies have a relatively even distribution in the world's population. However, this preference (unlike the other three preferences we will explore) has an unequal distribution, which is quite fascinating. According to the MBTI Manual, approximately three out of every four people prefer sensing, resulting in only one out of four people preferring intuition.

As a result of this, there can often be evidence of a societal preference towards sensing. In the United States, for example, I would argue that there is a clear bias in our education system for the sensing preference. The ways that we most often teach, develop curriculum, and assess learning are rooted in the sensing preference. Many of our standardized assessments require students to recall and remember facts and memorize sequential orders of events.

I would also argue that the United States business world prefers sensing over intuition. We have a tendency to value the hard facts, black and white data, focusing on variables that can be quantified and measured. Agendas presented in a sequential and predictable structure are valued in the modern business landscape of many industrialized nations.

The preference of intuition is most often favored in creative fields and sometimes in higher education. However, the vast majority of the way our world operates is rooted in the sensing preferences.

Knowing that the other dichotomies have a much more even split, it causes me to explore the reasons why this is the way it is. This makes me think of the famous question, "Which came first, the chicken or the egg?" This leads to the question: because our education and business structures are rooted in sensing, is that the reason the majority of people prefer sensing over intuition? Or do we socialize people to prefer sensing over intuition as a result of the way our education and business structures are designed? . . . Which came first?

I bring this up because I think it's important to recognize the distribution that exists in the world's population. Knowing this is critical when exploring how to overcome doubt by first recognizing a potential cause behind the doubt in the first place, which is what we will explore next.

How Knowing This Can Overcome Doubt

The big goal of this book is for you to understand how your individual uniqueness can help you overcome doubt. Specifically when looking at changes and transitions, it's critical to look at how you understand or take in information. As you examine changing variables or circumstances in your life, you will need to think about your thinking.

Before moving on ... take a second to stop and think. How do you most naturally prefer to take in information to understand the world around you? What type of information do you most often trust or feel comfortable receiving?

By recognizing the type of information that you prefer to take in, you will be able to identify the patterns in how you prefer to understand the world around you. Think about the power in that alone. We are constantly taking in new information, and by explicitly thinking about the mental process occurring within you, you can be more intentional when this occurs. This heightened intentionality will liberate you to seek out information that you're most comfortable with, increasing your confidence in making important life decisions.

Knowing your preference here will allow you to seek out and feed your brain the type of information it prefers, based off of how you're naturally wired. There is limitless potential in this alone ... so take the time to dive in to understanding how you prefer to receive or take in information. When you are faced with making a choice, you are often going to inform your decision. Knowing how you naturally prefer to receive information will help you to prepare for that critical choice prior to making a decision.

If You Prefer Sensing ...

You are naturally seeking information that is concrete and factual, and you will be drawn to focus in on the details. You are likely to use past experiences to make sense of the present reality. You have an uncanny ability to be centered in the here and now to take in the world around you using your five senses—what is it that you are hearing, feeling, smelling, tasting, and seeing?

In your twenties and thirties, you will likely be encountering the unknown frequently. What will tomorrow bring? Where are you heading? Your natural ability to utilize the past to understand the present may result in you feeling stuck because the idea of the unknown in the future freezes you from being your best. This will likely cause you to doubt decisions because dreaming about future possibilities is not how you most naturally understand the world around you.

Instead of letting the unknown of the future cause your mind to spiral out of control, take the reigns of the way you think and understand by giving your brain the type of information it is most comfortable with. Your mind will thank you when you feed it information that is concrete, detail-oriented, and focused on previous experiences of yourself and others.

Your brain will be at ease when it has the information it most naturally trusts. Let your brain focus on the black and white facts and the things that are in your control. It will not allow you to be the best version of yourself if your brain is being consumed by all of the unknown possibilities of the future that are not within your particular locus of control. Give your brain what it naturally craves, and it will help you gain confidence as you experience the world around you.

If You Prefer Intuition . . .

You are naturally seeking information that is abstract, theoretical, and focused on the bigger picture. You are likely to be oriented to think about future possibilities. You have the ability to see patterns and connections that will allow you to derive the themes and the meaning behind events in your life. Your brain may naturally crave to understand the outer world by considering the same event from a variety of different perspectives.

In this phase of life change and transition, you will likely be encountering something new. The vast majority of the people in the world will focus on the tried-and-true methods that have worked in the past. You will likely be inundated with concrete pieces of information. Too much detail-oriented information might actually freeze your brain from its best state of being.

Instead of overwhelming your brain with everything that occurred in the past and with concrete and factual pieces of information, do yourself a favor by giving yourself the freedom to focus on the bigger picture and the themes behind what's occurring in your life. Your brain will thank you when you allow yourself to think about the ideas and possibilities of what could be in the next phase of your life. If you haven't already, experimenting with simply trusting your gut or your "sixth sense" will be a valuable exercise for you.

Your brain will be at ease when it can understand the world in a way that it naturally prefers. Let yourself focus on the symbols, patterns, or relationships in what you're experiencing in this phase of your life. By not focusing too much on the details first, your brain will be able to internalize the big picture. Focus on the big picture, the vision, or the meaning first, and the details second. Give your brain what it naturally craves by taking some time to dream about future possibilities and what could be.

Overall

Again, you're going to use both sensing and intuition every single day. However, knowing what you most naturally prefer can liberate you to use your uniqueness to overcome when times are tough. When you're experiencing change and transitions, you can experience an increased level of stress in your life. This is when knowing the way that you naturally understand the world around you can help you to give yourself what you need to truly gain understanding.

Knowing that doubt is the lack of balance between your inner and outer worlds, this chapter is essential to conquering doubt. When you are receiving information about a choice you have encountered, the world may demand different types of information from you, or it might try to inform your decisions with information that you do not naturally prefer. Knowing your natural preference will allow you to maintain a greater degree of balance by giving your brain the kind of information you prefer.

Stop & Think

1. When do you see yourself using the "sensing" preference to understand the world? When is it limiting? When is it helpful?

2. When do you see yourself using the "intuition" preference to understand the world? When is it limiting? When is it helpful?

3. Think of a time when you were doubting a choice regarding a change occurring in your life. What type of information did you use to enlighten your decision? How could different types of information influence the process?

A Story of Choice

Enjoy the following thoughts from Jason C. (age 25), sharing when he experiences doubt and when he's at his best by maintaining balance.

Doubt in the Wild

Going through occupational therapy graduate school, it was really easy to feel like I was an imposter. I felt strong self-doubt like I didn't have the skills to be successful as a professional. It became almost automatic to compare myself to others in my program. During this time I really questioned whether I made the right decision about my career. I now know that this is where I'm meant to be but still have instances of self-doubt creep up.

Discover You at Your Best

I feel I am at my best when what I am doing is truly making a difference. Although I am in a helping profession, it is hard for me to always feel like what I do matters. However, when I notice a problem I can solve that will truly alter the life of someone else, I feel energized. Times like this are often when others have tried to solve the problem, but have missed subtleties in communication. I especially feel I am at my best when there is no clear answer. I really enjoy challenging others to see things a different way. These moments make me feel like I as an individual matter and there is something special about me.

Additionally, I feel my best when I am connected to a strong group of peers. This all may also be related to my need for genuine connection.

Reflections from Gary

Go look at how Jason experienced doubt again. He stated he doubted his skills, was comparing himself to others, and questioning his decisions. I imagine you can relate to this as well. Jason acknowledged this idea of "imposter syndrome" that appears a lot in young professionals. Doubt experienced in educational settings can often be rooted in the dichotomy we discussed in this last chapter, how you receive information. In formal learning environments, if the content is not being taught in a way that's easy for your brain to understand, it often causes you to think you're not in the right place. On the flip side, he experiences a strong sense of purpose when he's able to explore possibilities to solve problems that change the lives of others. Let's continue to overcome doubt together by looking at things in a different way!

CHAPTER 8

Choice

Let's connect some of the pieces that we've discussed thus far. We know that doubt is a lack of balance between your inner and outer worlds. Our bodies often signal to us that we are experiencing a lack of balance through strains, i.e., our responses to stressors in our lives.

One common stressor for twenty- or thirty-year olds are the many changes and transitions you encounter during this time period of your life. You often find yourself sitting at a fork in the road. You have to make a choice about what path you will take. In this chapter, we are going to explore a critical innate preference: your natural preference for making decisions and coming to conclusions in your life, the third of the four dichotomies.

Decision-Making

Have you ever thought about what you consider while making decisions? In the face of change and transition, decision-making is prevalent for many individuals experiencing doubt.

We are going to dive into two different styles that will describe your individual preference for making decisions. Again, just like previously explored topics, it is likely that parts of both preferences will resonate with you. You will use both of the options, but one is the path that feels more comfortable and the path you most frequently travel down.

Our goal is to ultimately decide which of the two preferences you rely on most often, feels most comfortable, or that you instinctively employ when making decisions and coming to conclusions.

Decide with Your Head Over Heart

The first group of people are those that prefer to make decisions and come to conclusions by taking an objective and logical approach. Someone close in my life that clearly demonstrates this preference is Matthew. He has an incredible ability to make decisions by looking at things from an objective point of view. When drawing conclusions, it is as if he is taking a step back from the midst of what is happening to analyze things from an outsider's point of view.

I notice that one of Matthew's gifts is being able to view things from a cause-and-effect perspective. While problem-solving, he is often seeking to identify the "root cause" of a problem or situation. Instead of simply looking at the outcome or the surface-level indications of what is occurring, he digs deep to understand the factors influencing the observed outcome.

Decide with Your Heart Over Head

The second group of people are those that prefer to make decisions and come to conclusions by considering personal priorities and the impact on other people. Another close friend of mine, Hannah, clearly demonstrates this preference. When she is making decisions, she has the ability to consider a situation from the perspectives of other people. When drawing conclusions, she does it by stepping into a situation from the perspective of the individual person who might be involved and takes an incredibly empathetic point of view.

I notice that one of Hannah's greatest gifts is valuing harmony between other people. While problem solving, she is often aiming to identify with the experiences of others and consider the values that will be reflected as a result of the decision. Instead of being detached from a situation, she is able to come to conclusions with a great sense of compassion and empathy for other people.

Thinking vs. Feeling

Remember . . . just as we previously discussed, parts of both of these preferences will likely resonate with you. However, one is likely to come with greater ease than the other. This sense of ease is ultimately what you are aiming to identify, as it will indicate which one you prefer.

Some people prefer to make decisions based on objective analysis. When drawing conclusions, it is more likely that this group of people will aim to analyze a situation. This preference is called thinking.

Some people prefer to make decisions based on personal values. When drawing conclusions, it is more likely that this group of people will aim to understand a situation. This preference is called feeling.

Again, don't just oversimplify these two preferences as logic and emotion—because everyone uses both logic and emotion on a daily basis. Everyone has the ability to think logically, and everyone has the ability to experience human emotion. To be very clear here, that's not the point that is being made. The key distinction is considering how you most naturally prefer to make decisions and draw conclusions using the explanations of each preference described.

The Cultural Bias

Considering biases in preferences is essential in order to help you identify what is truly your most natural preference, and not a behavior that you learned as a result of societal values or norms. When diving deeper into the thinking and feeling preferences, there is often a strong bias based off of the gender of an individual.

Broadly speaking, the majority of men identify with a preference of thinking, and the majority of women identify with a preference of feeling.

This bias in how decisions are made and conclusions are drawn is not necessarily biological in nature. Although some might make the claim that there are different hormones that are causing this preference to be skewed, I am not fully sold that this is true. For instance, over time the strength of this bias has decreased. According to the MBTI Manual, the thinking and feeling skewed results between men and women respectively, used to be nearly a 75/25 split. However, today we are seeking a shift closer to 60/40, and I have not seen any evidence in a biological shift in the hormones between men and women.

This leads me to believe that this is an environmental influence causing human beings to *learn* the behavior and values socially acceptable for their gender. Growing up, young boys and girls are socialized based on gender norms. Even if there are learned behaviors (nurture), every individual still has an innate preference. I would argue that there has been significant progress made in neutralizing some of these gender norms. However, at least in the United States, there is still much more work to be done in this arena from my perspective.

If you are a man who prefers feeling over thinking, you're liking going to encounter some degree of tension between your natural way of operating and the expectations the world traditionally has placed on men. The same is true for a woman who prefers thinking over feeling. These societal expectations can make you as an individual feel a sense of doubt because your natural way of operating is not in line with the traditional norms placed upon men and women in most parts of the world.

At least in the United States, sometimes men who prefer feeling are considered "soft" and women who prefer thinking are considered "cold." Quite frankly, our culture has developed even harsher terminology to describe men and women operating outside of gender norms, but I'll allow you to discover that explicit language on your own.

Recognizing this cultural bias and identifying your individual preferences can sometimes be liberating for men and women who are operating outside of traditional gender norms. There is absolutely nothing wrong with men who prefer feeling and women who prefer thinking. However, expectations from society can sometimes cause an imbalance between the expectations in the outer world and the natural preferences of your inner world. I encourage you to reflect on not what the world expects from you, but what your natural preferences are. When you identify your true natural preferences that exist in your inner world, you will create a greater sense of balance between your inner and outer worlds.

How Knowing This Can Overcome Doubt

This book's ultimate goal is to support you in the process of overcoming self-doubt, especially in times of change and transition. I would argue one of the best ways to do this is to gain clarity in your natural preferences of who you are as a human being in your inner world in order to navigate the expectations of others in the outer world.

Knowing how it is that you make decisions and come to conclusions can be critical in your quest to increase your own self-awareness. Using your individual uniqueness to combat doubt can help you to see the patterns of behavior that are most natural for you. The goal in this section is for you to first identify which preference is easier or more natural for you and to then apply that to live a much more balanced life between your inner and outer worlds.

Imagine if you knew how your brain was naturally attempting to come to conclusions and make decisions in the world around you. To take a minute to stop and think about the process that's occurring internally can be invaluable to see the pattern that's taking place each time you're making a decision or coming to a conclusion. Knowing this can help you to be more intentional in *how* you're making those decisions, instead of letting your brain subconsciously do its thing. Additionally, it's also important to note that others will be making decisions differently than you, and that's okay.

If You Prefer Thinking . . .

You have a natural ability to consider decisions from an objective point of view. You likely have the ability to temporarily detach from your emotions to consider decisions from an "outsider's" point of view in order to draw conclusions from an impersonal perspective. You may be drawn to logical reasoning and analysis in order to make decisions on how to proceed.

When encountering changes and transitions, you will likely need to draw conclusions and make decisions on how to proceed frequently. If there's a lack of balance between how your inner world operates in decision-making and what's occurring in your outer world, you may find yourself becoming frozen or feeling stuck when attempting to make a decision. It's quite possible that other people in your life may try to instill their own personal values upon you or try to make you consider the impact of others.

You may even feel tension between your natural preference of logical and objective analysis of a situation, and the impact that it may have on others or your own inner values.

In times of stress, you will likely experience a tension between your usual objective approach to life and an increase in emotion. This tension can manifest itself in a variety of ways, but you may begin to feel a rush of negative emotion internally or it's possible that you could even lash out at others externally. You might even become incredibly defensive or find yourself frozen and feeling indecisive and unable to move forward.

To "snap out" of this, it's critical to get back to the way that you prefer to naturally operate. It's essential to not allow the thoughts and feelings of other people to consume your mind. You will need to find a way to get connected back to the objective and logical analysis that allows you to draw conclusions regarding the world around you in the healthiest way possible. By doing so, you'll be able to allow your mind to focus in on the way you most naturally prefer to make decisions, instead of letting the stress of the situation take you off course to use the feeling preference that is less dominant for you.

If You Prefer Feeling . . .

You have a natural ability to consider decisions from an empathetic or value-based point of view. You likely have the ability to lean into the emotions of not only yourself, but also others, in order to consider decisions from the perspective of those who may be impacted by a particular decision.

In times of change and transition, you will likely be making many decisions and drawing a lot of conclusions. If there's a lack of balance between your internal preference for decision-making and what the world expects of you, you may paralyze yourself from making any decision at all. It's quite possible that other people in your life are constantly feeding you the facts and pushing you to use logical analysis to form your conclusions and make a decision.

You may feel a tension between your natural preference of considering values and the desire of other people to interpret things primarily through a logical and objective analysis.

In times of stress, it's likely that this tension may cause you to initially try and make decisions by analyzing the facts and taking an objective approach—counter to your natural way of operating. This tension may result in you becoming cynical, criticizing yourself and others, or detaching yourself in a way that's unhealthy due to your natural preferences. You might even find yourself becoming cold or pessimistic about the decision that you need to make in your life.

To "snap out" of this, it's critical to get back to the way that you prefer to naturally operate. It's essential to not let the world's desire to make decisions based off of logical analysis overcome your natural ability to take a personal and empathetic approach to decision-making. You will need to find a way to get centered in your personal values or how your decision impacts other people in order to make a decision out of the best version of yourself. By focusing on your natural process for drawing conclusions and making decisions, you can operate out of the "true" version of who you are, instead of letting the stress of a situation take you off course to use the thinking preference that is less dominant for you.

Overall

Remember that every single person has access to, and uses, both thinking and feeling. The goal is for you to identify your natural preference—which preference is easier or more comfortable for you to make decisions and draw conclusions? When you're experiencing change and transition in your life, you will absolutely be making a lot of critical life decisions. By knowing the process that you most naturally prefer to utilize internally to draw conclusions and make decisions, you can be more intentional about the way you operate in the world.

Instead of your mind subconsciously making decisions, you can consider the things that are most important to you personally as an individual and focus in on the process that works for *you*. There will always be people in your world that are operating out of a different perspective, and although they can provide a new angle to the decision you are making, you must remember that you are the author of your own story. The narrative is up to you, and *you* ultimately must make the choice.

Use this information to know the process you prefer to utilize. Then, use that understanding to create a better sense of balance in your inner world when you need to make a choice. Increasing the understanding of your inner world will give you the confidence to make choices based off of who you innately are. When these choices start to become more clear, the series of choices over time will help you choose your best life.

Stop & Think

1. Think about a major life decision you made recently. How did you ultimately make the decision?

2. When do you find yourself naturally using the thinking preference versus the feeling preference?

3. When in your life have you seen a cultural bias influence your own behavior?

A Story of Choice

Enjoy the following reflections from Trisha F. (age 25), sharing when she experiences doubt and when she's at her best by communicating to cultivate strong relationships.

Doubt in the Wild

Anytime I've had a transition in my life it has sparked anxiety and doubt for me. Whether it has been a new job, a new home, a new friend group, or a change in routine, I've found myself doubting who I am and who I want to be. For the first few years of my career I was teaching in two separate buildings—the middle school and the high school. I had the opportunity this year to teach in one building instead of two, and for some reason I was struggling with the idea of change. I wanted my life to be less stressful and "easier," but I was doubting whether I could be successful in teaching upper level students (something I had never done) and whether it was actually what I should do. I was also worried about leaving my coworkers that had become close friends.

Discover You at Your Best

I am at my best when I am working with others. I truly believe that my outgoing and friendly personality allows me to connect with people of all ages and backgrounds. I've always been told I can have a conversation with anyone, so I constantly seek out opportunities to build connections and relationships with others through conversation. As a teacher, I use this every day to connect with students, colleagues, administration, and parents. Though I am a young professional, my communicative strengths have been something I can use to allow people to get to know me as a teacher, colleague, and friend.

Reflections from Gary

Trisha was faced with some big decisions in her career that sparked a lot of doubt. It sounds like working through these decisions was a challenge, a challenge that many people can relate to. It can be incredibly hard to overcome the pressure that is often paralyzing when we are faced with major life decisions. It is evident that Trisha prefers "feeling" as discussed in this chapter, and she was hesitant to leave her job partially due to the relationships she built. Thinking about how having a reduced workload could give her more time, she realized she could maintain existing relationships with previous coworkers. Just as we discussed in this last chapter, maintaining a healthy balance when making decisions is so important to choose your best life!

CHAPTER 9

Structure

Structure in the Outer World

The final dichotomy looks at how you tend to visibly behave in the outer world, especially when looking at structure. By this, we are looking at the way that you extravert your behavior. All people will have a balance of both preferences, but the challenge is to determine which one you prefer to visibly display to others.

When you look at the world, maybe you see decisions that need to be made and desire to create order. Or, maybe you see a world that needs to be explored and experienced. In this chapter, we are going to look at how you are more comfortable approaching the outer world. Don't forget, every single person will use both of the preferences, but one will be more comfortable than the other.

The Planned and Scheduled Approach

The first group of people prefer to live a much more structured life that is full of order and is well-planned. A close friend of mine, Melissa, is great at developing a structured plan for both the long term and short term.

When working on a longer-term college paper, she would begin the process by identifying when she wanted to complete the project and develop a detailed timeline of what she needed to accomplish and by what deadlines. She would begin planning and outlining at the beginning of the process, in the first week of receiving the assignment, and then continue to make measurable progress week after week. She would produce a rough draft, re-read her work, think about the approach she took, and make some final edits, until ultimately submitting the high-quality paper a few days before the deadline.

In this example, Melissa appears to take an organized approach to accomplish this task. Day by day, she would make measurable progress. Her approach was designed to ideally avoid any last-minute stress as the deadline approached.

The Spontaneous and Adaptable Approach

The second group of people prefer to live a much more open life that tends to be spontaneous and adaptable. A close friend of mine named Justin is great at exploring options and is much more comfortable keeping things open to allow for flexibility.

When working on the same long-term college paper, he would begin the process by reading the guidelines given by our professor and then thinking about the many options. Justin would not begin actually producing the assignment on paper until a few days before the paper was due, but would spend a considerable amount of time thinking about how he might ideally approach the paper. He would have a large spurt of energy as the deadline approached and develop a high-quality assignment that he submitted at the deadline.

In this example, it appears that Justin took a much more casual approach and aimed to make final decisions as the deadline approached. Although he did not produce the assignment until close to the deadline, he spent time and energy exploring options leading up to the deadline. His approach was designed to ideally take advantage of the energy he experienced as the deadline approached.

Judging vs. Perceiving

There are parts of both Melissa and Justin that I'm sure resonate with you. Depending on the context, I'm sure you've experienced both. However, one process is likely to be much more comfortable for you and result in less stress for you. This will be a good indication of your natural preference.

Some people prefer that the outer world is organized and orderly, ultimately seeking for decisions to be made. This preference is called judging. To be clear, this does not mean you are judgmental towards others; it simply is the term used to describe this preference, which originated from Myers and Briggs.

Other people prefer to experience the world, ultimately seeking options that need to be explored. This preference is called perceiving. To be clear, this does not mean that you are perceptive necessarily. Again this is just the term used to describe this preference.

It is also worth noting that this dichotomy was not originally included in the framework of Carl Jung. This dichotomy was later introduced by Myers and Briggs as a way to illustrate the way that you use some of your other preferences. This is often referred to as type dynamics, cognitive functions, or mental processes of individuals. I like to explain this as how your mind is wired.

This book is not designed to go in depth into the cognitive function or the wiring of your mind, as it can get incredibly intricate for each of the sixteen individual types in the Myers Briggs Type Indicator. I would ultimately recommend getting connected with a MBTI Certified Practitioner through The Myers & Briggs Foundation to learn more about your individual cognitive functions.

The Lazy Misconception

Different cultures have different inherent biases for how individuals approach the outer world. I've noticed that in the United States, our society values the judging preference. If you look at the way our society is structured, having a well-thought-out plan in advance is generally preferred. Using a very concrete example, most people prefer agendas set for meetings ahead of time. Although this could be an indication of a judging preference, this isn't a clear indication of this preference at all.

I have repeatedly heard that perceiving types are simply lazy... or that P stands for procrastination. This misconception is typically due to the fact that perceiving types receive a burst of energy as a deadline quickly approaches, which many often interpret as being lazy or late all the time. Simply put, this is an immature understanding of this preference. Healthy people with a preference of judging or perceiving are both fully capable of creating plans and meeting deadlines; the major difference is in the *process* or *how* the task will be completed.

How Knowing This Can Overcome Doubt

The ultimate goal of this book is to help you overcome self-doubt, especially in times of change and transition. By understanding your natural preferences, you can maintain a better balance between your natural internal preferences and how you show up in the outer world.

Understanding this dichotomy can be particularly helpful because it begins to illustrate how you show up in the outer world. Knowing how you naturally show up in the outer world will allow you to begin to understand how the perceptions of other people may influence you.

The reality is we will all experience deadlines, but we live out different processes in *how* we approach meeting these deadlines. The observable behavior may be different than what you are experiencing internally, and that's perfectly okay.

For example, if you consider an approaching deadline at work or school, it may be the perception of others that you haven't started working on it at all. However, it may be likely that you've been thinking about it internally, considering different options, and thinking about different ways to approach the task. Other people may think that you're not working hard or that you're procrastinating, when in reality you are thinking about it all the time, but you haven't started to execute on producing the deliverable.

Understanding this fourth preference will help you understand how the perceptions of others (in the outer world) may be causing you tension in how you naturally perceive your internal process towards structure (in your inner world).

If You Prefer Judging

You have a natural ability to take a planned and scheduled approach to life. You likely approach a deadline in a streamlined manner that supports incremental progress along the way.

As a result of your preference for judging over perceiving, it is likely that in times of change and transition you prefer to make a decision efficiently.

It is likely that making a decision will help you avoid stress by avoiding game time decisions. Naturally, you are less likely to revisit a decision that you might have previously made. You may find that making a decision allows you to free up headspace or mental capacity to do other things.

In most circumstances, your natural ability to plan ahead and having things decided will allow you to live confidently. However, it is possible that you may still encounter doubt after you have made a decision.

Closure is important to you. It's possible for all types to make a decision too soon, but those who prefer judging over perceiving may experience doubt as a result of making a plan too far in advance. After you make a decision, you may start wondering what "could be" or what other options existed. You may begin to think about other possibilities.

It is important to first recognize your preference for making a plan and having closure in your decision-making processes. If this is true for you, you might find yourself looking back on the decisions you've made and wondering if you did the right thing. Being aware of how you approach the outer world can allow you to see your natural preference for having decisions be made and allow you to act more confidently out of your natural preferences.

If You Prefer Perceiving

You have a natural ability to be open, spontaneous, and adaptable. You likely receive a burst of energy as a deadline approaches that causes you to execute as time goes on.

As a result of your preference for perceiving over judging, it is likely that in times of change and transition you remain open to whatever decision you might need to make until the deadline is near.

It is likely that leaving the door open, without making a decision too soon, allows you to explore many different options in the various decisions you might need to make. You may find that the ability to "explore" the world around you is your natural inclination.

In most circumstances, this will be very helpful and likely be the way that you prefer to operate in the world. In times of stress, however, it is likely that this exact preference to be open to other possibilities may be causing you to doubt yourself.

Have you ever heard of FOMO? It's the fear of missing out. It's possible for all types to experience it, but those who prefer perceiving are likely to experience it as a result of waiting until there is time pressure in order to make a decision. It is possible that P types do not want to miss out on anything in life and want to be able to explore all possibilities before making a final decision.

It is critical to first recognize your likelihood to explore all possibilities. If this is true for you, be aware that this may actually cause you to experience self-doubt. Being aware about how you approach the outer world can be liberating in order to allow yourself to think about how you might show up to others in this facet of your life.

Overall

Ultimately, there are two key things you can do to help yourself maintain a healthy life in this regard. The first is to be aware of your natural preference between judging and perceiving. The second is to maintain a healthy balance in the way that you see, think, and operate in the world.

We all have access to both of these preferences. Knowing how you likely show up in the outer world is critical to help you overcome doubt and live a confident and balanced life. Remember, this is all about how you show up in your outer world. By recognizing how you show up in the outer world, you can begin to reflect on the balance between your inner and outer worlds—the ultimate strategy to conquer a sense of self-doubt.

By knowing how you most naturally prefer to operate in the world, you'll be able to see the patterns in your behavior to balance your inner preferences with the way you are operating in the outer world.

Stop & Think

1. Picture a long-term project you've worked on in your life. What is your most natural approach to getting it done?

2. Imagine taking an approach that's the exact opposite to getting the project completed. When would you use this style to structure your approach? What would you typically experience internally?

3. When was a moment you've experienced FOMO recently? How did it influence your approach?

A Story of Choice

Enjoy the following thoughts from Nick L. (age 26), sharing when he experiences doubt and when he's at his best by staying organized and keeping measurable goals.

Doubt in the Wild

This was a time of great doubt for me: nearing the end of college, about to graduate with no plan. But all of my friends knew exactly what the were going to do—either had a job lined up or going to specialized grad school.

Discover You at Your Best

When I feel organized, I'm at my best. At work, I feel most organized and ready to lead others when I feel that I know exactly what my measurable goals are for the day, week, and month. Then, I take the steps necessary (normally by making to-do lists) to achieve those goals and meet deadlines.

Reflections from Gary

This is a perfect illustration of tension in how Nick was showing up in the outer world, just as we discussed in this chapter. Nick recognized that he had no plan as graduation was approaching, which often sparks doubt for students and recent graduates. It also sounds like Nick was comparing himself to his friends that had a clear plans of what was next after graduation, which likely sparked an even greater sense of doubt. On the flip side, Nick indicates that feeling organized and having measurable goals allows him to be at his best. Let's continue to overcome doubt by balancing how we show up in the outer world!

CHAPTER 10

Synergy

You're Greater Than Your Four Preferences

In this book, we've taken a look at four different parts of an individual's personality. Using the original work of Carl Jung, which was later developed by Katharine Briggs and Isabel Myers, we have looked at what is commonly known today as the Myers-Briggs Type Indicator.

By looking at each of the four dichotomies, you have already begun to gain a baseline understanding of the eight different preferences that make up this system. However, the power of this system really begins when you understand how the four different preferences work together in your life. These four preferences working together create your unique "personality type," which is one of the sixteen types created as a combination of the various preferences within this framework.

In this chapter, we are going to look at how knowing your individual preferences is just the beginning of understanding your uniqueness. First, you will explore how your individual preferences can combine to create your personality type. Second, you will begin to discover that there is a deeper layer in this framework to help you understand why you do what you do. Third, you will also begin to see how the preferences, when combined together, create a much more intricate picture of your unique personality by looking at pairs of preferences combined together.

This chapter is illustrating the concept of synergy—when the interaction of individual parts results in a combined effect greater than the sum of the individual parts—that is occurring within you. The entirety of your unique personality type cannot be accurately defined by just four simple letters. However, the interaction of those four letters begins to create a much more holistic illustration of your uniqueness when you begin to see how they combine together.

The Sixteen Personality Types

By first examining each of your four preferences outlined over the last four chapters of this book, you will begin to understand your personality type. Each of the preferences within the four dichotomies can be represented by a single letter.

Energy	(E) Extraversion	(I) Introversion
Understanding	(S) Sensing	(N) Intuition
Choice	(T) Thinking	(F) Feeling
Structure	(J) Judging	(P) Perceiving

Using the MBTI assessment tool as a framework, your personality type is a four-letter code that represents your innate preferences. The letters of your type are always presented in the same order as we discussed in this book, and only one preference is selected from each dichotomy. There are sixteen possible personality types represented by the letters listed above for each preference (such as ESTJ, INFP, ENTP, etc.). Your personality type is a beginning point to explain how you see, think, and operate in our world—your individual uniqueness!

Type Table–The Sixteen Types

ISTJ	ISFJ	INFJ	INTJ
ISTP	ISFP	INFP	INTP
ESTP	ESFP	ENFP	ENTP
ESTJ	ESFJ	ENFJ	ENTJ

By simply looking at each of the four preferences in isolation (for example, E vs. I), you're only beginning to see a baseline understanding of what makes you unique. Looking at how you refuel and recharge your energy is just one aspect of your uniqueness. However, by putting all four of the preferences together as your personality type (for example, ESFJ), you are starting to understand how you see, think, and operate in our world at a much greater level of depth.

The preferences, when working together, will begin to codify and show patterns of behavior, or the unique personality, of an individual. When you are not operating out of your unique personality, this is when you experience imbalance, thus doubt. This will be much more fruitful in understanding your individual uniqueness than just looking at your individual preferences in isolation.

During the process of becoming a certified Myers-Briggs Practitioner, the ethical use of the instrument was a key part of the training. During the training experience, it was emphasized that you should first know your individual preferences by using the "official" instrument and by working with a practitioner to go through an interactive feedback session.

In order to construct the actual Myers-Briggs Type Indicator, there have been many statistical tests to verify the reliability and validity of the tool. This is ultimately why I encourage you to utilize the official instrument, and not free versions that are readily available online. The free versions that have become popular on the internet are not legitimate and may not give you results that are accurate.

Although it can be insightful to read descriptions of the sixteen types, I do not intend to include those descriptions in this book. It is important that individuals have an understanding of their individual type before studying the descriptions. The actual descriptions of this instrument have been crafted by researchers over a period of decades. Although it can be fun to read the various descriptions of the sixteen types that can be found all over the internet, many of those descriptions are not rooted in the authentic instrument.

If you're intrigued by the content described throughout this book, I would encourage you to work with a certified Myers-Briggs Practitioner to learn more about your psychological type. This person will help you verify your type while also helping you to see the deeper layers of your individual uniqueness. This will ensure that the information you are receiving is a product of decades of research and is coming from a reliable source.

The Wiring of Your Mind

After you've identified your personality type, or the four-letter code made up of your natural preferences, you can start to understand why you do the things that you do. The Myers-Briggs Type Indicator goes much more in depth to understand an individual's personality beyond the individual preferences (e.g., E vs. I) or even your personality type (e.g., ESFJ).

There's a deeper layer than just knowing your personality type, and that is to understand your cognitive functions. I refer to this as the wiring of your mind. When simply looking at the dichotomies of a person, you are generally looking at the behaviors exhibited by a person. However, the cognitive functions explain *why* those behaviors are occurring.

One analogy for understanding the cognitive functions is to imagine a four passenger vehicle inside of your mind. I first learned of this analogy, known as the Car Model, from Joel Mark Witt and Antonia Dodge at Personality Hacker. In the Car Model, there are four passengers (inside of your mind) that are influencing your behavior.

Of those four passengers, there is one that is dominant or has most of the control, and that's the one in the driver's seat. This is the part of your personality that people will most often attribute to who you are. Next, there is a co-pilot. The co-pilot helps to provide some balance to the driver by helping you navigate and see how you can best navigate obstacles that might be thrown your way. However, the driver is mostly in control, and the co-pilot is simply there to advise.

The driver and the co-pilot are the parts of your personality that are most evident and the strongest parts of who you are. However, there are two more passengers inside of your mind. In the backseat, you will find two kids—a ten-year-old and a three-year-old. These two kids are not the strongest parts of your personality but will still impact the way that you show up in the world.

Each of the sixteen personality types has their own unique order of cognitive functions—or the passengers in the car. By learning more about this, you will have the ability to understand the way that your mind operates. This is ultimately what's causing your behavior.

Due to the fact that each of the sixteen types has their own unique wiring of the mind, I will not go into the details of each type. I would not be able to describe the cognitive functions inside of this book with due diligence; however, as already mentioned, I would encourage you to learn more about them in partnership with a Myers-Briggs Certified Practitioner. This layer of understanding will go beyond just codifying your behaviors, but truly allow you to see *why* you do the things that you do.

My goal in this section of the book is for you to know that there is a deeper layer in this framework than just understanding your own individual preferences. You are so much more than just the four individual preferences described in this book. Those preferences, however, begin to paint a picture of the natural way you operate.

By using this baseline understanding, you can begin to uncover even greater depths of who you are than what could be simply described in this book. This greater level of depth can allow you to understand what's causing your behavior and more about your unique way of thinking. By discovering more about the uniqueness of your inner world, you can create a better degree of balance in your life—therefore, conquering self-doubt.

Function Pairs

Another way to begin seeing how the whole is greater than the sum of the individual preferences is to begin looking at the function pairs within this framework. As already expressed, when looking at your personality type, there is a sequence of four letters that make up your type. When looking at function pairs, you are simply looking at the middle two letters of your personality type (S vs. N and T vs. F). This creates four sets of function pairs: ST, SF, NF, and NT.

When looking at the function pairs, it's important to first remember what each of the preferences are describing. The first dichotomy described in the function pair examines how you understand or take in information—sensing and intuition. The second dichotomy in the function pair examines how you make decisions—thinking and feeling.

Function pairs are easily identifiable on the "Type Table" illustrated above. Function pairs are simply the columns in the table. Within each of the four function pairs, there are four personality types included in that grouping.

Function Pairs–Columns of Type Table

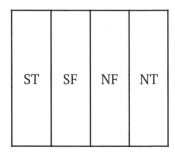

According to the MBTI Manual, Isabel Myers saw an incredible amount of power in function pairs to know the cognitive style of individuals. The synergy created between these two preferences has proven to be helpful with career interests, which we'll look at in a general way in the upcoming brief descriptions of the four function pairs. Remember, this is one way to generalize the sixteen types into four different groups.

Please note that the names of each of the following function pairs and parts of each description have been constructed using data provided in the MBTI Manual.

ST: The Practical and Matter-of-Fact Types

The four ST types (ISTJ, ISTP, ESTP, and ESTJ) are known for their preferences of sensing and thinking. As a result, STs often thrive in areas that involve concrete information and logical analysis.

The MBTI Manual suggests that ST types are drawn to "economics, law, surgery, business, accounting, production, and the handling of machines and materials."

SF: The Sympathetic and Friendly Types

The four SF types (ISFJ, ISFP, ESFP, and ESFJ) are known for their preferences of sensing and feeling. As a result, SFs often prefer understanding concrete information through their senses and are often more subjective in their decision-making.

The MBTI Manual indicates that SF types are particularly valuable in "service-with-a-smile jobs, teaching (especially in the early grades and applied fields), nursing, pediatrics, and other health fields involving direct patient care."

NF: The Enthusiastic and Insightful Types

The four NF types (INFJ, INFP, ENFP, and ENFJ) are known for their preferences of intuition and feeling. As a result, NFs are often drawn to communicating the possibilities they see and the values that those possibilities are attached to.

According to the MBTI Manual, NF types are particularly "attracted to work that involves the unfolding of possibilities, especially possibilities for people, such as in teaching (particularly in the upper grades and college), selling intangibles, counseling, writing, and research."

NT: The Logical and Ingenious Types

The four NT types (INTJ, INTP, ENTP, and ENTJ) are known for their preferences of intuition and thinking. These often means that NTs focus on possibilities and logical analysis.

The MBTI Manual states that NT types "are best in solving problems within their field of special interest, whether scientific research, mathematics, the more intricate aspects of finance, or any sort of pioneering or innovative endeavor in a wide variety of technical or administrative areas."

Am I Supposed to Be a Nurse?

Now, there's one thing I want to make very clear. Does the above information mean that all nurses are SF types? Absolutely not. Or if you're an SF, does that mean you should be a nurse? Not necessarily. The goal of looking at function pairs is to categorize people into groups based off of common preferences.

I believe that any healthy, well-balanced, and well-developed individual can do any job. However, there are some jobs that may naturally be better aligned for different types of people.

I know for a fact that there are nurses in our world representing all of the sixteen individual types. I'm also certain that there are nurses of all sixteen types that enjoy their line of work and are satisfied with their lives.

However, knowing your type will help you recognize the natural way you operate, which will help you choose your best life.

Overall

By now, I hope that you're beginning to see that this book is just the beginning. The goal of this book is to explore how each of the four dichotomies and the framework developed by Jung, Myers, and Briggs can be used to support self-discovery to conquer self-doubt. However, there is a whole lot more that this tool can do.

If you are enjoying this journey so far, I would encourage you to explore the greater depths of this framework by discovering your type and beginning to explore your cognitive functions. You are so much more than just four letters of a personality type, but those four simple letters can start to uncover even greater discoveries to help you see the uniqueness of your inner world. The synergy formed by the combination of the individual parts of who you are is what allows your individual uniqueness to take form.

Stop & Think

1. There are four pairs of preferences. Identify one of each pair that best identifies your natural preferences.

    E vs. I

    S vs. N

    T vs. F

    J vs. P

2. Which of the four function pairs does your type fall into? What resonates with you about the brief description of the function pair?

3. If you choose to continue the journey to learn more about your inner world and your individual uniqueness using your personality type, what do you still want to learn and discover? *(Hint: you might consider exploring areas of frustration or moments of conflict in your life.)*

A Story of Choice

Enjoy the following thoughts from Brett H. (age 28), sharing when he experiences doubt and when he's at his best by focusing on growth.

Doubt in the Wild

I experienced doubt when I was making the transition last fall from a business I'd run and loved for years, but was feeling complacent with, to deciding to look for opportunity in a new industry without any concrete plan. I made the decision to transition out of that role with nothing in place other than a half-hearted confidence that I would figure it out. It was the fear of the unknown. I feared landing in a role that was less engaging and growth-focused as before out of the necessity to pay the bills, and not doing something that I could truly thrive in. I'd only saved up enough money to get me through three months before I had to find something, and I doubted my skill set and connections at times would be enough. However, it was actually both of those things that landed me with my new company.

Discover You at Your Best

I'm at my best when I'm surrounded by sincere and genuine people—people that want to have deep conversations. I'm at my best when I can work with others that are open to growth just as much as me—that will allow me to speak into that growth-orientation and that will give me an internal feeling of serving and helping them. I love making people laugh, so I am at my best when I feel comfortable enough with the people around me to add a comedic spin to the dialogue.

In a different flavor, I feel like I am at my best when I am building something while learning and advancing my skills simultaneously:

working on cars and writing/producing music have always put me in this flow state where I'm competent enough in the skill to not get discouraged, but not skilled enough yet where the learning is still constantly exciting. I feel like that's the sweet spot for leaning into my creativity and my learning too. I also feel like I'm at my best when I have the headspace to do exercises like this—introspection fills me up.

Reflections from Gary

Transitioning from one job to another often sparks doubt in people. Brett is certainly not alone in this experience! Notice how when Brett is at his best, he focuses in on growth, creativity, and balance. Just as we discussed in this chapter, there's so much more to Brett as a human being than just his four preferences in isolation. Looking at how those four preferences work together begins to create a much richer explanation of what's occurring in Brett's inner world. Let's continue to follow in Brett's footsteps by discovering the complexities of what makes us each unique in our inner worlds.

CHAPTER 11

What's Next?

Understand Individual Uniqueness to Overcome Doubt

In this chapter, I want to do two things. First, I want to review a couple of the major points made throughout this book in order to draw some final conclusions and "connect the dots" between some of the points made in this book. Second, I want to guide you through some next steps to continue to learn about who you are as an individual.

The number one goal of this book is to help you overcome a sense of self-doubt. This book has taken a very specific approach to making this a reality. First, let's review that doubt is a lack of balance between your inner and outer worlds. Shifting your focus too much internally or externally will cause you to feel overwhelmed, begin questioning everything, and cause you to be frozen from uncertainty and the fear of the known.

This place of self-doubt is usually quite negative, and most of us don't want to spend too much time there because it paralyzes us from living the best and most authentic version of our lives.

To conquer self-doubt, or the lack of balance between your inner and outer world, it's essential to create a better sense of balance. The following three ideas make up the model presented in this book. I would challenge you to move from self-doubt to choosing your best life by embracing the following:

1. You must first increase your understanding of who you are as an **individual** and what makes you **unique**. Using tools like the Myers-Briggs Type Indicator (MBTI) is one way to begin this journey.

2. By understanding your individual uniqueness, you will then be able to enhance the **balance** between your **inner** and **outer** worlds. By applying your new understanding of your inner world, you will ultimately be able to make choices using your own potential as the measuring stick of success, instead of the expectations of the outer world.

3. When you experience a healthy balance between your inner and outer worlds, you'll then be able to move away from experiencing **self-doubt.** In moments of change, transition, and important life decisions, you will instead feel empowered to choose your best life, by making choices that are in alignment with your unique wiring and your natural preferences. These series of choices will allow you to live an

authentic, meaningful, and balanced lifestyle that you were meant to live.

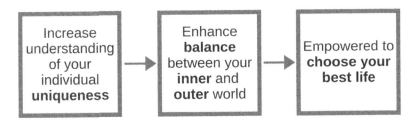

Your Individual Uniqueness

In this book, we used the framework originally developed by Carl Jung in *Psychological Types* that was later developed into the Myers-Briggs Type Indicator to help you have a structure to see your individual uniqueness. This book is just the beginning to see how your uniqueness can help you to overcome self-doubt to, instead, making a series of choices that will result in you choosing your best life. If you haven't already, I'd encourage you to explore your individual preferences to find which of the sixteen types aligns with your natural preferences.

Knowing your individual type will not only allow you to grasp an understanding of your individual preferences, but also of your cognitive functions. Your cognitive functions will help you to understand how your mind is uniquely wired.

Understanding your uniqueness will allow you to stop comparing yourself to the outer world (resulting in doubt) and, instead, compare yourself to your own unique potential. By understanding what makes you unique, you can bring balance into your life and live life with a lens of adventure. This balance is critical to living your best life, and why would you want to settle for anything less?

Balancing Your Inner and Outer Worlds

Every single person has access to both their inner world and the outer world. In the framework discussed throughout this book, those with a natural preference for introversion generally prefer to direct energy to the inner world. In contrast, those people with a natural preference of extraversion generally prefer to direct energy to the outer world.

Seeing where you most naturally direct your energy will help you to first embrace your natural preference. This will help you to identify where you may need to be intentional in directing your energy in order to create a healthy balance.

As discussed previously, doubt is experienced in the inner world and triggered by things in the outer world. By identifying the sources of what is sparking doubt and knowing about your individual uniqueness, you can ultimately maintain a healthy balance between your inner world (operating out of your uniqueness and natural preferences) and outer world (of interacting with other people and events).

By knowing your unique way of seeing, thinking, and acting in the world, you can take action with confidence by measuring up your life to your own potential, instead of to the lives of others.

Choose Your Best Life

Once you've grasped what makes you unique, you can focus to create a healthy balance between your inner and outer world using your natural preferences. This will then allow you to shift your mindset when you begin to experience doubt. Your awareness of experiencing doubt is the first step, but recognizing what is triggering it will allow you to make choices in alignment with who you naturally are.

If you first identify what is triggering you to compare yourself to others, becoming overwhelmed by uncertainty, or getting stuck on negative experiences in your past, you can then begin to identify how to shift your mindset. By recognizing the negative pattern that is occurring within you internally, you will be able to "rewrite" the messaging that's occurring within your mind to a much more positive pattern.

In her book, *Find Your Thing*, author Lisa Zelenak states, "How you see your situation changes everything." This directly relates to what we discussed earlier in the power of perception. How you choose to interpret stressors will ultimately impact your self-concept. You can choose to create this positive shift towards an internal locus of control by recognizing the variables you can influence—and you can always influence your perception and interpretation of the outer world.

Now, let me be real for a moment. This will not happen overnight. If you are frequently experiencing a repetitive negative pattern of thinking in your mind, you may not instantly switch it to a positive message. It may require thought, reflection, and processing to break this cycle. However, it is possible. By knowing your uniqueness, you will be able to see how your mind is wired and be able to take action from a place that you know is true and authentic to who you are. Instead of allowing the outer world to spark a negative sense of doubt internally, you can allow the outer world to spark a positive sense of adventure.

I am confident that you can move from doubt to adventure. Doubt freezes, isolates, and restricts us from excellence. Is this really the space that you want to stay in? The fact that you made the choice to pick up this book and read through to the end is evidence that you're seeking something more.

You have a burning desire inside of you to live life with a lens of adventure. Imagine a life that you are excited about living, a life that feels energizing, a life that allows you to thrive. This is the life that I want to choose. I know that you can make the choice to live your best and most authentic life. Is this the choice you're going to make?

Proof of Concept

Earlier in this book, we examined some examples of when people experienced doubt in their twenties and thirties collected from the survey I conducted. One of the first moments of doubt we explored came from Sam.

> *I feel like I am constantly in doubt. Especially in college, I always wondered if what I was doing was the path that was best for me. Now that I am in a specific career, I wonder about my future in this career, when to start a family, etc.*
>
> —Sam N. (age 25)

Based off of Sam's experience in college, she was able to focus on making one choice at a time to choose the life she wanted to live. Sam's natural preferences align with the personality type INFJ, and she soon discovered her natural desire to empower others. She started her professional journey as a teacher and then made the choice to return to school for a doctorate degree in psychology. She is now excited about the possibilities of her future as she is making choices that align with her inner world. She's able to work with people but at a pace and setting more in tune with her preference of introversion. She's able to bring hope and empowerment to others, something that her function pair of NF will thrive on. This is the power of making choices based off of the uniqueness expressed in your inner world.

We also explored an example of when Erica experienced doubt.

> *Motherhood. Every day is a new doubt. Am I doing it "right"? Will he grow up to be a respectful man? Will he ever sleep through the night? Am I setting him up for failure? Will he meet all of his milestones? Am I cut out for this?! The list goes on and on...*

—Erica V. (age 25)

Based off of Erica's experience in motherhood, it sounds like she wants the very best for her son. There will likely be times in the future that Erica questions her parenting decisions, but by discovering her uniqueness in her inner world, she is intentional in the choices she makes for her son. Erica's natural preferences align with the personality type ESFJ. Knowing this, Erica naturally is someone who selflessly puts the needs of others before her own. Erica made the choice to become a social worker, a profession that allows her SF function pair to thrive. The SF pair is known as being sympathetic and friendly, and her profession of choice is a great avenue to live this out. By recognizing her natural preferences, Erica can realize that her greatest source of self-doubt is actually her greatest strength in this instance. Erica relentlessly pursues meeting the needs of others, and it is inherent in who she is. Seeing this gives her a greater degree of confidence in the choices she is making for her son on a daily basis.

Community

As human beings, we are social creatures. No matter if you prefer introversion or extraversion, we were meant to coexist in community with others. As you continue this work of moving from doubt to adventure, I would encourage you to find a community of people to be able to have meaningful dialogue with. Maybe this is a friend or family member. Maybe this is a significant other or spouse. Maybe this is a trusted colleague at work. Maybe this is a boss. Or maybe you've hired a professional coach or counselor. Whoever this person might be, it may help you to have a conversation about your experience with doubt and most importantly about your individual uniqueness.

Sometimes the easiest way to see your uniqueness is to examine who you are from the perspective of another person. The people who love you the most and see your potential can sometimes see what makes you unique with great clarity. Here is one of my favorite stories that perfectly exemplifies this concept:

> *There are these two young fish swimming along, and they happen to meet an older fish swimming the other way, who nods at them and says, "Morning, boys. How's the water?" And the two young fish swim on for a bit, and then eventually one of them looks over at the other and goes, "What the hell is water?"*
>
> —Original Author Unknown

In this story, the two young fish have no idea what water is. To the human being, as an outsider, it's very clear that fish are surrounded by water as they are swimming. However, as a fish, this is the norm and it's all they've ever known. They've never experienced life without water and, therefore, cannot see this obvious truth.

This can be connected to us as individual human beings. Sometimes, we are unaware of the things that make us unique because we've only ever truly experienced our own lives. The way that you think, feel, understand, process, and interact with others is all that you've ever known. Sometimes we can see the uniqueness in others before we can see the uniqueness in ourselves.

This exemplifies the importance of community. Sometimes, we may not see something in ourselves that is blatantly obvious to others. By staying connected to others that we know and trust, we are able to have difficult conversations about things that we might not even see. By articulating what you're experiencing internally and how it's impacting the balance of your inner and outer world, you'll be able to increase your sense of understanding and have someone outside of yourself for a layer of accountability.

Continuous Journey

The reality is, there's always more to learn about you, yourself, your uniqueness, balancing your inner and outer worlds, and moving from doubt to adventure. Ultimately, I want to invite you on this continuous journey. There will never be a clear ending in this journey of knowing yourself, creating balance between your inner and outer worlds, and ultimately shifting from doubt to adventure. The good news is, you can make the choice to begin this continuous journey now.

Will this book conquer every moment that you may experience doubt for the rest of your life? Unfortunately, no. However, by considering your uniqueness, I am confident that you can begin to create a better sense of balance in your life. This balance will ultimately let you have ownership over the narrative of self-doubt you experience within your mind.

Two of my previous managers influenced me through a simple phrase to help create a shift in my mindset. This phrase is just three simple words, "I used to . . ." This phrase begins to create separation in your mind of your old way of doing things and will help you shift your mind to a new narrative.

As a college student and student employee within my college residence hall, I was overwhelmed with learning the names of four hundred other students that I interacted with on a daily basis. My boss and mentor gave some tips and tricks to help me learn names, but one of the biggest things that needed to change was my mindset. I would often say, "I'm bad at names." This set me up for failure right from the beginning. Instead, I was challenged to say, "I used to be bad at remembering names, but I'm getting better at it."

This simple phrase demonstrates how our thoughts and language can influence our performance. The original narrative in my mind was rooted in my past failures. The original narrative was stuck in a limiting belief that prevented me from being my best. When I was open to shifting my mindset, I was able to begin learning names faster than ever.

This same shift can occur when you look at moving from self-doubt to choosing your best life. The outer world can spark doubt within you, but *you* have the power to shift the narrative. You will always have the ability to interpret the outer world with a negative lens. This will ultimately result in doubt. However, the opposite is also true. In every moment, of every day, you have the ability to shift your perspective starting with your inner world of your uniqueness to operate out of confidence. This will allow you to shift from doubt to adventure.

This mindshift is the beginning. You have the power to shift your mindset. You must explore your uniqueness. You must choose to create balance in the midst of chaos. You can make the choice . . . no one else can choose for you.

Instead of seeing the outer world and getting stuck in comparison, I challenge you to begin this journey of working from the inside out. Know yourself and your uniqueness first, and then continue to create balance. This is a continuous journey. You have the power to choose your narrative and to choose your best life.

References & Resources

Briggs Myers, I., Kirby, L. K., & Myers, K. D. (2015). *Introduction to Myers-Briggs® Type: A Guide to Understanding Your Results on the MBTI Assessment* (Seventh ed., Introduction to Myers-Briggs Type Series). Sunnyvale, CA: CPP.

Briggs Myers, I., McCaulley, M. H., Quenk, N. L., & Hammer, A. L. (2003). *MBTI Manual: A Guide to the Development and Use of the Myers-Briggs Type Indicator Instrument* (Third ed.). Mountain View, CA: CPP.

Institute for the Future. The Next Era of Human Machine Partnerships: Emerging Technologies' Impact on Society & Work in 2030. (2017).

Jung, C. G. (1971). *Psychological Types*. Princeton University Press.

Schwartz, B. (2004). *The Paradox of Choice: Why More Is Less*. New York: Harper Collins.

The Myers & Briggs Foundation. (n.d.). Retrieved from https://www.myersbriggs.org/.

United States Department of Labor, Bureau of Labor Statistics. (2018, April 17). Retrieved from https://www.bls.gov/news.release/nlsyth.nr0.htm.

Witt, J. M., & Dodge, A. (2018). *Personality Hacker: Harness the Power of Your Personality Type to Transform Your Work, Relationships, and Life*. Berkeley, CA: Ulysses Press.

Witt, J. M., & Dodge, A. (n.d.). Personality Hacker: Personal Development Using Personality Models. Retrieved from https://personalityhacker.com/.

Zelenak, L. (2018). *Find Your Thing: Escape Monotony in Your Mid-20's & Do Work That Matters*. Publisher: Author.

Notes & Key Ideas:

Notes & Key Ideas:

Notes & Key Ideas:

Notes & Key Ideas:

Notes & Key Ideas:

Notes & Key Ideas:

Notes & Key Ideas:

Notes & Key Ideas:

About the Author

From Michigan to Tanzania, from the education system to the non-profit sector, Gary continually works to influence others to live with purpose. Being fueled by his fascination of individuals' uniqueness, everything he does is to inspire others to stop and think so that they can imagine a better future for our world.

In between runs along the Detroit Riverwalk, Gary likes to spend time with his pup, Chip, named after the Central Michigan University Chippewas where he formally studied psychology, communication, leadership, and education.

Gary wears many hats—he has served in a leadership development non-profit, supported teachers as an instructional coach, and developed curriculum for personal development organizations. Now, Gary coaches others to find an authentic way to share their story with the world to create an impact on the lives of others.

Learn more about Gary's story and how you can imagine a better future for our world at: www.betterfuturecoaching.com.

Can You Help?

Thank You for Reading My Book!

I really appreciate all of your feedback, and I love hearing what you have to say.

Please leave an **honest review on Amazon** letting me know what you thought of the book.

Amazon reviews will help me know what you thought of this book and help other people decide if this is a good book for them!

Thanks so much!

Gary Williams

Made in the USA
Columbia, SC
08 February 2021